"As a colleague of Bill's for many years, I know that he is a kind, compassionate, and forthright clinician. He also possesses the kind of wit that redirects stale perspective, which is always the sign of a great teacher. A conversation with Bill is an adventure, and I have been lucky to have had many of them. Now, through this book, everyone will get to sit down with Bill and learn from a man who has been through life-threatening challenges and has gleaned from them not only wisdom but joy. How lucky are we to be able to benefit from his experience!"

—Julia Forth, Author, Speaker, Chief Executive Officer, Cancer Support Community

"You would be lucky to know Bill, but if you don't, read his book! He is extraordinary, with a persona that exudes rare authenticity, kindness, and *joie de vivre* derived from a remarkable, almost unbelievable life journey. Bridging myriad subcultures ranging from the rural Midwest to the South to the West Coast, from the warm embrace of a large, close-knit extended family to the chilly outlands of addiction and chronic disease, from the paternalistic ways of the past to the more inclusive milieu of today, he unites impactful life experiences into a profoundly singular life story revealing unmined dimensions of our shared humanity. His is a story that grips us, releases us with empathy and humor, and ultimately changes our outlook on others."

—Eileen Monnin-Kirby, Senior Resource Management Consultant, The World Bank

"Bill Kavanagh is a gifted therapist. His book is full of hard earned practical wisdom which can benefit anyone who has, in his words, reached a "fork in the road" of life. Through his own life's lessons, he teaches us all about a "new normal," a normal, whether secret or open, that that can help us turn tragedy into victory, one that can help us to grow and to blossom, and to embrace our "authentic self." As his subtitle says, life is about "finding joy after life's challenges."

—Bill Aron, Author, Photographer

Keep Your Fork! Something Sweet is Coming
by Bill Kavanagh, LMFT

ISBN 978-1-64663-955-7

Published by

◣köehlerbooks™

3705 Shore Drive
Virginia Beach, VA 23455

800-435-4811

Keep Your Fork!

something
sweet
is
coming

⊙ ⊙ ⊙

FINDING JOY
AFTER LIFE'S CHALLENGES

Bill Kavanagh, LMFT

VIRGINIA BEACH
CAPE CHARLES

DISCLAIMER

This book is not intended as a substitute for psychotherapy or counseling, nor should it be used to diagnose or treat any medical or psychological condition. The reader should regularly consult a physician or therapist in matters relating to his/her health and well-being. This book is designed to provide information, motivation, and guidance to its reader. The content of this book is the sole expression and opinion of its author. The author shall not be liable for any physical, psychological, emotional, or spiritual outcomes.

I dedicate this book to my father, Joseph John Kavanagh,
to my mother, Nancy Ann Ryan Kavanagh,
and to my amazing siblings, Cecelia, Eileen,
and the twinses, Kathleen and Kevin.

Table of Contents

Introduction

Are you struggling to overcome a challenge? Are you craving new meaning in some aspect of your life? Are you simply feeling stuck? You might answer yes to all three.

For those who have reached a fork in the road and need to make *some* kind of choice, why not choose to discover new excitement in the sweet possibilities of that process? That's exactly what this book is all about. It's meant to inspire you to come to grips with what you're dealing with by embracing the challenge while expanding your toolkit to help you cope and flourish in a new comfort zone.

I will lead you through many of my own personal struggles. Some of my story is uncomfortable to read, and hopefully some of it will make you laugh, as humor is one of my favorite tools for dealing with pain, loss, and fear. I think my foibles and follies can help you figure out how to handle all kinds of issues.

Picture a cartoon showing a newborn baby emerging from the womb. He rubs his eyes, looks up at the doctor and utters two words. "Now what?"

Confusion, uncertainty, and anxiety can occur at any time and at any age and become downright insidious and painful. Experts in human behavior have long theorized that being squeezed from our mother's uterus is one of the most traumatic incidents of our lifetime. Everything as we formerly knew it is suddenly gone. Those months of calm and quiet, sheltered in the lazy, guilt-free privacy of the womb, is ripped away when a doctor's cold rubber glove grabs us and pulls us into the glaring light of harsh reality.

This moment of birth hints at what is to come: a series of constant disruptions that lurch and wrench us out of our comfort zone. Is it fair? It doesn't matter; that's just the way things go. Is *life* fair? Of course not, and that is the best gift we could have. After all, if our quality of life was fully determined by our own comfort, we would never leave the womb, and then what would we do with all the shower presents and those adorable onesies?

Let's take that scenario one step further. As a newborn, we instantly become one of the most beautiful gifts a mother and father could ever imagine. We are tenderly wrapped up in a warm, soft blanket and loved by everyone who holds us. This shocking and unfamiliar situation is the beginning of love and life. Imagine that. Had we never left the womb, we would never experience love. Or Disneyland. Or sushi. Or Netflix.

Being forced out of our comfort zone can be a glorious gift, and childbirth is our first proof of that. But do not disregard the difficulty. When faced with any horribly uncomfortable situation, go ahead and scream and cry as hard as you possibly can, just like you did on your original birthday. That type of behavior is natural and even necessary. As if to add insult to injury, just when you think the trauma has passed, someone slaps you on the ass. Finally, when you're well swaddled and hear one of your parents singing a sweet lullaby, you can finally relax. The stress is over; except it's not—at least, not until the fat lady sings.

We all encounter struggles. They might arrive in the form of an illness, a divorce, the death of a loved one, a job loss, an addiction, or pick a struggle, any struggle. They're no picnic.

The healing process includes grief, acceptance, and moving forward. When it comes to moving forward, it's important to remember that doing so is a choice. When we reach a fork in the road, we can try to return to the life we had, which may no longer be available, or we can change lanes and begin a new way of thinking. That usually begins with an exploration of why the struggle originally happened. Digging for answers often prompts a few central questions:

- What was the trauma meant to bring into my life?
- Why did this happen?
- What am I supposed to learn from it?

In my case, I've had more practice than I ever thought necessary in dealing with traumatic challenges, beginning with losing my mother at age seven, being bullied in school, coming out as gay, navigating the AIDS crisis, facing up to addiction, battling cancer, and shall I go on?

In every trauma I've faced, finding a blessing has been an option—maybe not at first, but eventually, when I was ready to allow them to enter my psyche. That requires a welcoming frame of mind, which we can choose or refuse.

The difficulties, of course, come without warning. The rewards come through discovering appropriate lessons and flourishing. If there's one basic thing I've learned, it's this: *Problems don't happen to us. They happen for us.*

So, when we reach any type of fork in the road, we can find unexpected excitement in the exploration of new paths, or we can choose to remain stuck. We can let a traumatic experience shut us down, or we can allow it to expand our character as we discover a new future.

Whether the new path is successful is never guaranteed. It could possibly lead to another fork in the road. The best part comes with following a new adventure, as doing so can provide hope all by itself. Hope requires positive thinking, and that suggests a huge step forward.

The road we choose to take will always include sudden stop signs and hidden curves. These roadblocks and detours are there for a reason. Sometimes, they are a result of societal norms and pressure—the "supposed to be" syndrome embedded in our brain by the time we reach adolescence. Behavioral factors also play a role. Our tendencies and habits are often the result of patterns we learned as a child. If that doesn't quite explain your predicament when you come to a fork in the road, consider factors like judgment, religion, ethical standards, and the opinions of others. They can scramble anyone's mind and impede progress, and if your brain tends to ramble like mine sometimes does, your path to peace may be even longer and more complicated.

Overthinking or overplanning, which inevitably become roadblocks for sensitive people, can also undermine the synchronicities that are handed to us for a reason. Ram Dass (1931–2019), the beloved spiritual healer and psychologist, described this dilemma beautifully. "A flower does not question its meaning or purpose, or its right to exist," he said. "It simply *is what it is*, and its purpose is joy."[1]

This approach suggests that in the exact moment when we are faced with unexpected change, our reaction defines who we are as human beings. *We* don't decide many of the changes in our life. *Life* decides.

Attaining happiness does not depend on learning how to create a perfect and rewarding life. It comes through a balance of creating and accepting, by blending our dreams with the cards we are dealt and always adapting to change. A delicate balance exists between the ability to design the life we want and the capacity to accept the life we are provided.

The key to happiness is in establishing that balance.

We create some of our own gifts, of course, and the universe provides its own, too. Some of them are more beautiful than we could ever design or expect. Yet we all know that many of the universe's gifts come wrapped in some damn shitty paper. Without question, many of the ugliest gifts end up being the most beautiful—if we allow them to be. And what we think will be beautiful gifts might end up being ugly.

After all, if we were always happy, we would never know we were happy.

---

1 Ram Dass, *Still Here: Embracing Aging, Changing, and Dying* (New York, NY: Riverhead Books, 2000).

We often forget that one of our most beautiful blessings is the freedom to pursue happiness, and that nothing can stop us from that pursuit. The key word is *pursue*. We must act in order to discover happiness. Once we find it, happiness can become part of our DNA. You see people every day, I hope, who have discovered it—laughing, falling, getting up, and laughing again. They can't wait for the next joke.

For most of us, true happiness will not come without a healthy dose of compassion and generosity. Compassion liberates everyone: the giver, the receiver, and those who witness it happening. I am a firm believer that we cannot be happy without generosity in our lives.

Viktor Frankl said, "It does not matter what we expect from life, but rather what life expects of us."[2] Although his book *Man's Search for Meaning* changed my life and I worship everything he has said, I believe our lives are a combination of what we expect and what life expects of us. Expectation can lead to goals, and goals can generate motivation, empathy, and happiness.

Frankl also said, "When we are no longer able to change a situation, we are challenged to change ourselves."

Those are the moments that define who we are. They change us one way or another, and we can make those changes valuable, meaningful, and impactful in our quest for purpose. Striving for meaning is as basic as our human craving for sex, love, and food. It is a deep inner desire to fill what Frankl calls an "existential vacuum."

All of the events in our life lead us to meaning. According to University of California researcher and author Sonja Lyubomirsky, "Forty percent of our capacity for happiness is within our power to change."[3]

---

2 Viktor, E. Frankl, *Man's Search For Meaning* (Boston, MA: Beacon Press, 1959).

3 Sonja Lyubomirsky, *The How of Happiness: A New Approach to Getting the Life You Want* (New York, NY: The Penguin Press, 2008).

The truth of happiness and the power of life lessons lie in the combined experience and their aftermath. Good or bad, what did you learn? What will be your attitude and the narrative you keep about the experience? How will you view your past and your future?

Change is not always comfortable, but it *is* inevitable. In that regard, we get hit, we get up, we move on, *and* we remember it in words. We create our own narrative by what we say and how we say it. This becomes our story. Each of us has one. How do we want to tell it? How do we want to be remembered as relating it?

We all quote our parents and grandparents. Might they be surprised at what we remember coming out of their mouths? Might *we* be surprised what others remember about us? We need to be conscious of how we talk about our lives. Words and attitude are important.

We will never remember an exact incident or experience. We will only remember the words we use to describe it. Our mood, our legacy, and our life are all about the language we use to record, digest, and express it. *The words we use.*

This book shares my personal journey and reflects on how I have dealt with those shittily wrapped gifts, those life moments that hit hard and without warning. I hope that some of the advice I share will help you overcome your own unique challenges. It's been generated from a variety of sources and wise people as well as from my experience and schooling in clinical psychology, along with discussions I have shared with hundreds of people on the subject of "What's next?"

My challenges with cancer, drug addiction, and AIDS have created plenty of physical pain, emotional distress, and psychological uncertainty. In the aftermath of the physical challenges, when I was finally healing, came the beginning of the real trauma. As you probably know, as much as we would love for life just to be normal again, it does not work that way. It's not a freaking Disney movie.

Any new life requires a death of some kind. Otherwise, it is not new. We must learn to accept that which has been taken away and find joy in new beginnings. Our hearts and minds are not so different than the gardens we keep. We must cultivate the soil, plant new seeds, and harvest what we can for our own nourishment and the benefit of others. It's a natural cycle of seasons and growth.

The title of this book is a metaphor based on the similarities of being at a crossroads in your life and the moments we live between courses in a meal. I don't know about you, but I love desserts, so this perspective always resonates. You finish one course and hold on to your fork, anticipating the next one.

Let's take the metaphor to another stage and see if you can define exactly where you are in your struggle by answering these questions:

1. *What is your empty plate?* What are you losing? What is being taken away from you?

2. *What is your fork?* What are you holding on to that you have previously learned? What gives you hope?

3. *What is your napkin?* Who and what can you count on to catch you if and when you fall?

4. *What is the dessert that is coming?* What is on the menu for your future?

These are the questions we will keep asking and trying to answer as the book unfolds. At the end of each chapter, you will find a "Mindful Moment," a chance to reflect on what's been presented, and the "Mental Gym," an exercise you can do to help you move forward. It might be useful to dedicate a notebook to responding to these sections.

"You either get bitter or you get better," says Josh Shipp, motivational speaker, author, and TV personality. "It's that simple. You either take what has been dealt to you and allow it to make you a better person, or you allow it to tear you down. The choice does not belong to fate; it belongs to you."[4]

This is your time. When you come to a roadblock where the delicious dinner is over and you think that nothing will ever taste good again, hang on to your fork. Read your menu. It's right there in front of you. There is still a wonderful sweet treat to come.

Throughout the book, as I describe each of my setbacks, I also explain those four elements of my healing—my answers to the questions raised above. There have been times when the waiter came back and told me that my dessert choice was no longer available, and I had to review the menu and find another way forward. He never took my fork from me, but I had to hold it a little longer than anticipated.

No one else can find your new life. There are always new roads to discover and explore, but only you get to find your rewards. Otherwise, they are not rewarding.

Now I invite you to step forward.

4 Josh Shipp, *Jump Ship: Ditch Your Dead-End Job and Turn Your Passion into a Profession* (New York, NY: St. Martin's Press, 2013).

CHAPTER 1

If Ya Ain't Doin' Too Good,
Don't Stay Too Long

I was the perfect little boy. "Straight" A student. Number one at penmanship in the state of Ohio. The class clown who made everyone laugh. I stayed after school and helped my teachers clean. I was a perfect little altar boy for the Catholic Church—so perfect I was awarded altar boy of the year two years in a row.

As if that weren't enough, I was pack leader for my Cub Scout troop and president of my 4-H gardening club. We were the "Ho Ho Hoers" until one of the mothers decided it was inappropriate to call her son a ho, much less a hoer. We became the Jolly Green Growers, and I was the jolliest of all. My strawberries and corn were stellar, but I won the Madison County Fair blue ribbon for my petunia baskets. That's right. Perfect petunia baskets. Isn't that the dream of every father, particularly one who played basketball and had a dream that his sons would be basketball stars?

Turns out, I misunderstood "basket." It didn't matter. I still have the ribbon to prove that my baskets with balls of petunias were perfect.

And then . . .

One day, when I was six years old, an older girl from down the street, Stephanie, came by, and I showed her the closet next to my bedroom to marvel over how perfect it was. The walls were made of cedar, a perfect place for my mother to keep all her fancy clothes from the past, including her wedding dress. We all knew the sacred power of the cedar closet.

Stephanie closed the door and told me we were going to play a game. She pulled out a bag of Red Hots and explained that we were going to take turns to see who could put the most Red Hots up the other's butt. She said it was our fun little secret game that no one else could know about. To make sure that no one did, we would put the Red Hots back in the bag after our game and return them to the kitchen.

Because I was not good at sports, I had never felt the ensuing adrenaline-rushing excitement. Secrets, though, gave me a rush. I felt like I had finally been chosen as a real teammate when Stephanie elected to play this game with me.

This began a long life of red-hot secrets. In fact, that is the definition of "in the closet," and for me, it literally began there. The "cedar closet" became the "secret closet."

But no one is perfect, and the more we try to be perfect, the more secrets we are hiding.

I was aware of some of the secrets, and some of them would later be revealed. As I have grown, matured, and explored the secrets throughout my life, I've learned that nothing fuels the adrenaline of a secret more than strengthening the opposite outer image. In other words, as a child, my secrets became even more hidden if I could be more perfect on the outside.

Later, as my secrets were forced out, I almost always got the same response: "Wow, Bill, I never would have known." In some way, that made my secret "successful."

Is that the goal? To have a successfully hidden secret?

ALWAYS BLOOMING

Let's look at it another way. Each of us is alone in our head. We have an endless number of daily conversations with ourselves. Every one of them is a secret to the rest of the world. It would never be possible to share those conversations with others. They come and go so quickly that we don't even have time to listen.

Secrets, however, go both ways. There are those we hide from others and the ones that life reveals to us. Just when we think we have discovered the hidden secrets, they become more of a mystery.

The true secret is what blooms from inside the secret. When that happens, life hands us a new mystery, and it's up to us to uncover it and discover what is inside.

As a child, striving to be perfect gave me my only sense of worth. I knew I was not like the other boys, and I wasn't like my role model—my father. I was different, and that felt wrong. Like so many other children, I felt shame for not fitting in or being able to be what I was "supposed" to be.

As it turned out, being "different" was the best gift I have ever been given. It was my first hint that struggling to find meaning or purpose meant taking a deep dive into exploring my true self and my soul. That is the only intention I needed back then and now. The singular secret I craved was my own identity.

Everything that happens to us turns into something to learn. Our lives are like a big scavenger hunt. We're given a small clue for how to get to the next step, and when we reach that step, we're presented with a new clue to take us a little further to another step. This way, we live an exciting journey, traveling from step to step—or for many of us, from secret to secret.

PERFECT LITTLE SINS

As a child, a big symbol for the justification of secrets was the Catholic Church's manner of disclosing and forgiving those secrets, also known as sins. The way to "confess" them and have them washed from my soul was to be squeezed into a small, dark space conveniently called a confessional. I would close the door and kneel in shame until I heard the sound of a tiny little door sliding right in front of my face. That's when I quietly whispered my plea for forgiveness.

"Bless me, Father, for I have sinned."

Basically, that was a formal way of saying, "Hey, dude, I've got some secrets. Can ya maybe do the deal and have them eliminated? Nobody has to know. Just you and me."

By the way, why don't drug dealers or mafia hit men use a confessional?

Never ever *ever* did I confess my real sinful secrets to the priest. There was not a chance (in hell?) that I would reveal my best secrets. "Umm. Stephanie and I put candy up our butts. You down with that? I'll say a couple of Hail Marys and we'll be cool, right?"

Instead, I made up perfect little sins. We all did.

"I lied to my teacher."

"I yelled at my sister."

"I stole a nickel from my father."

I loved the balance of perfection and secrets. Yet there is no such thing as perfection, and there are no true secrets. I secretly was perfect at proving both statements.

PLANTING SEEDS, KEEPING SECRETS

One big secret changed my life. Late in the summer of 1962, when I was seven, my mother took me to the store to buy lilac seeds.

"Let's have a secret," she said, "just you and me. We'll plant these seeds along the garage, and then in the spring they will start to grow, and after a while, they will bloom. We can say 'Surprise!' to the rest of the family."

I loved flowers and couldn't wait to see them grow and make everyone happy. Four months later, however, my passion and excitement were turned upside down in what seemed like one incredibly unfair life secret.

Early on New Year's Day, my four siblings and I woke to the unexpected sound of aunts and uncles mumbling quietly downstairs in our living room. One by one, as we crept down the steps, Dad led us into his bedroom, where he closed the door and said the words.

"Kids."

He put his head down and took a long pause.

"Last night, your mommy went to heaven."

And then he sobbed uncontrollably.

It was the first time I had ever seen him cry. That was more disturbing to me than the news he was telling us. My seven-year-old brain could not process the concept of death, but I felt my father's pain and fear. My two older sisters also began to cry. I had learned appropriate behaviors from my father, so something told me that I should also be crying, but I didn't know why. At that moment, I had not heard that Mommy would not be coming home, that she would never speak to us again. I would never be able to lay my head on her lap for comfort and love. All I heard was that she was visiting heaven.

"Daddy, does she still love us?"

That made him cry even harder.

"Yes!" he said quietly and loudly at the same time. "*Yes.*"

My mother had been ill for a while. She suffered from Addison's disease, which had forced her to be in bed often, but her death came as a complete surprise to everyone. While Dad was cleaning the kitchen and her five children were asleep upstairs, she died peacefully alone in her bed. Earlier in the night, my oldest sister, Cece, was in bed with her. Mom told her to go up to her own bed, and as Cece was leaving the room, Mom told her that she loved us and our father very much. Those were her last words. Cece remembers hearing Mom take a deep breath, which now she believes might have been her last.

As our aunts and uncles came into the room and took us in their arms, and my father's brother, Uncle Eugene, took Dad into another room, one huge thought began to haunt me.

What about our secret?

Mom had told me that the lilacs would eventually grow into beautiful and fragrant purple flowers, and they would be our gift to the family.

What do I do with this secret?

Thus began the script for my entire future.

REDEFINING NORMAL

As Dad proved to me over and over, we live in a heteronormative, male-dominated culture. *Norm* is the key syllable in that word, and I was not normal. Ironically, I look at society today and laugh at the thought of my being normal. Praise the Baby Jesus that I am not normal. Each difficult lesson that made me feel different and alone became another step toward making me unique and my own individual. There is no question that our greatest assets and our most cherished gifts come from our most difficult struggles and challenges.

There has never been a year that winter has not turned into a beautiful spring. There has never been a day that darkness didn't turn into light. We can always find hope in the cold, dark secrets that are unveiled to us.

What if we were more acutely aware of the blessings that might arise when something forces us to begin a tremendous test of our strength? Those blessings take us further from the boring world of normal. It is those tests and lessons that define who we are. They mold our character and make each of us a special piece of non-boring, *ab*normal art.

It is also vitally important to be mindful of the feelings and emotions that occur while going through those life lessons. That's where the secrets are hidden. That is our path to discover the good secrets, the ones that are life-affirming.

No matter what societal dialogue might teach us, we are not automatically required to pull ourselves up by our bootstraps and go on. Tough transitions and unexpected twists will always occur. To block those events or the emotions they create would prevent some of the most significant times of our lives from happening, as well as our most powerful learning opportunities.

Struggles can become our most beautiful souvenirs.

Behind the beautiful Walt Disney Concert Hall in downtown Los Angeles is an outdoor garden with a large fountain in the shape of a rose, dedicated to Lillian Disney. The fountain is constructed from broken pieces of Delft china, from her huge collection of antique dishes. The architect, Frank Gehry, named the fountain *A Rose for Lilly*. It is a beautiful piece of art created from the broken pieces of her past. To me, it represents how we can take all of our unique, life-defining moments and reform them into an entirely new piece of art. The only requirement is to make that choice. Otherwise, the pieces remain in ruin.

Just as I didn't know what would bloom when my mother and I planted those seeds, we also never know what we can create when we least expect it.

MY ROAD TO TRAVEL

Secrets can excite us and haunt us. I was a little gay boy living a secret I would not even reveal to myself for another fifteen years. More years would pass before I recognized that the secret with my mother was not about what was going to bloom in our yard but rather what would eventually "bloom" in the aftermath of this tragedy. It was about my life *and* the garden. They were one and the same. My mother had planted the seeds, with my little hands helping, and no one knew what would eventually bloom.

It is miraculous that my first lesson in fearing the future, along with the complete confusion of a secret, was taught to me unconsciously by my mother. She knew that I was trying hard to hide my not being like the other little boys behind a mask, and I believe she knew more than

I did about my identity. She was an exceptionally loving and protective mother and provided unlimited comfort. She was my shield. There was no doubt that I needed to grow into a more dependent and mature person, but her death seemed like an awfully cruel way of ensuring that I did.

I was already introverted and shy, and losing her made it ten times worse. Suddenly, there was no one who understood me. For a time, any desire for perfection came to a halt. My grades plummeted. I was constantly dazed and confused, lost and alone, though my oldest sister would have done anything to help me, and two of my aunts, Dottie and Sally, both stepped up to help Dad raise five sad and lonely children.

My aunt Dottie became one of our saviors. She let us kids come and stay with her for several weekends, giving Dad a chance to grieve on his own. One time, while all of my siblings were in her living room, I decided to explore the upstairs of this beautiful large home, beginning with "the library." Dottie and her husband, Uncle Eugene, were school administrators, so they owned an endless number of books. I decided to spin around in a circle, stop, and point at a random book. I opened it to a random page, and pointed my finger at a line in the book and memorized it. Then I went down to the kitchen where Aunt Dottie was cooking and recited the line.

"Aunt Dottie, when I grow up, I am going to choose the road less traveled."

She froze, turned off the stove, put both arms around me, and started to cry.

"You absolutely will, Billy. You absolutely will. And that will allow you to be the special person that you are."

I had no clue what she was talking about; I had no clue what "the road less traveled" even meant. However, because she was so moved by it, I never forgot it. Of all the books in the library, and the millions of lines I could have selected, I miraculously chose that line to memorize. Thank you, Aunt Dottie.

Since she also told me that I had a talent for writing and art, I wrote and illustrated my first book at the age of nine. She helped me send it to Dr. Seuss, who responded with a two-page, handwritten letter encouraging me to write and draw. That letter remains an enormous impetus for me to express myself, and it inspired me to embrace a loving gift for myself and my family in the stories I invariably wrote depicting my childhood.

The lilacs were beginning to bloom.

"IF YA AIN'T DOIN' TOO GOOD, DON'T STAY TOO LONG"

My father died in 2007. He endured the frontline trauma of World War II, two heart attacks, Parkinson's disease, and the deaths of three wives. He earned a degree in agricultural engineering, but he spent most of his career in real estate.

He grew up on a farm in central Ohio, and one of his favorite childhood tough-luck stories involved subzero temperatures, hungry farm animals, and ice-cold hands. He told us that some days he had to stop and beat them on the side of the barn to keep them from freezing. Then he would always laugh and say, "My hands, not the farm animals."

His stories had good, solid morals attached to them, usually about working hard in the face of obstacles. "Get the job done and get it done right" was his lifelong motto. His stories made me who I am. They molded how I think and work, and they illustrate all the ingredients that helped to shape me personally, ethically, and professionally.

Between mother number one and mother number two, Dad struggled with raising five children while maintaining his career. He did not have a lot of money, so he walked the streets of our home city of Columbus, knocking on doors to find a housekeeper to stay with us during the week. That's when Lena Bond entered our lives. She had just returned from a national tour for Quaker Oats, portraying Aunt

Jemima. We literally had the logo living with us, cooking for us, and comforting us Monday through Friday.

Lena never ate with us—not by Dad's direction, but by her own. However, one night while serving dinner, she overheard one of Dad's tough-luck stories. She stopped and put her hands on her hips.

"Mr. Joe," she said, "my daddy always told me that if ya ain't doin' too good, don't stay too long."

Dad laughed through the entire dinner, and Lena's words, which perfectly summarized his philosophy to stop worrying and move on, became another ongoing motto.

When I graduated from eighth grade, Dad was our commencement speaker. I have no idea why I remember his speech. Probably because I was terrified of being embarrassed, so I listened harder than anyone else in the audience. His speech carried a beautiful message of moving forward in life and captured everything I hope this book will convey.

Dad ended by saying that life is like a ladder. We must continually climb. Sometimes, we will slip a few rungs, and sometimes we will have a strong foothold and move up with a steady pace, always saying yes to whatever challenges we face.

"But while standing on each one of those rungs," he said, "if ya ain't doin' too good, don't stay too long."

A LITTLE LOVE GOES A LONG WAY

As I write, I am on an airplane. The pilot just announced that we are about to encounter a dark, cloudy, bumpy ride.

"Sit back and relax. We'll be through this shortly, and when it's over, you're going to see a beautiful sky on the horizon."

Some people are closing their window shades, while others are opening them. It is an amazing metaphor for how each of us chooses to see life, present and future, afraid or excited.

It is such a gift to always look for the beautiful sky on the horizon.

A common misconception is that we are weak if we're not that tough guy who can just "get over it." Simply getting your ass back out on the field is not the way most people succeed in overcoming a difficult challenge. A little love and understanding can go a long way. Our sports-minded culture of screaming at failures implies that there is no compassion in mistakes.

My friend Tom Cushman is an Olympic coach. He shared a life-changing discovery about how he became a successful coach. It began when he recognized that most people need a little understanding and compassion.

"They need to hear, 'I believe in you,'" he said. "We need to ask, 'What can we both do to make your skill better?' That comes a long way from, 'Get your ass out there on the field and do what I tell you!'"

We often confuse self-compassion, self-worth, and self-esteem. When something difficult happens, we immediately compare our situation to others'. Suddenly, we're not perfect. We are now "less than." That is exactly when we need self-compassion. There will always be others in a better situation, and there will always be others dealing with something worse. It doesn't matter.

Comparison is the opposite of compassion.

In today's world of Facebookology, comparison is easier and more ubiquitous than ever before. Every time we check in, we see others enjoying and loving life. It is difficult to not get wound up in FOMO (fear of missing out) and feel like everyone else is having more fun than you are.

Turn it off and call a friend or a loved one. Instead of screen time, make it scream time!

Be good to yourself. When we love ourselves and have compassion for our problems, we are demonstrating love, which is healing and can turn into courage. Compassion for the world can only begin with compassion in our hearts for ourselves. As they advise on airplanes, put your own oxygen mask on first. Learn to feel your feelings in depth and have compassion for yourself, or you will never have space for genuine compassion for others.

THE JOY OF "WHY?"

One of the reasons *The Wizard of Oz* has resonated with so many people is because it is a simple story of a tragedy that forces Dorothy into an entirely new, magical world that she would have never discovered without being literally thrown into it.

What we seek, what we dream of discovering, is hidden inside of us.

We sometimes need a difficult reason to display our strength, our love, our inherent intelligence, and our passion. The movie beautifully shows how we can overcome a challenge by engaging with a community of characters who can walk with us down that yellow brick road. Together, we can teach each other courage, help reframe our brains, and go deep into our hearts.

Just like lilacs, life blooms in extraordinary and beautiful moments that happen when we least expect them. Time stops as we glow in the surprise of the magic. Those moments confirm that we are stepping in the right direction. When we act with sincerity, and when we act with honesty and goodness, everything we do is right, and life will bloom in a moment of joy.

I mentioned in the introduction that throughout the book, as I examine my struggles, I will convey four elements that turn them into potential lessons:

1. What was my empty plate? In other words, what was taken away from me?

2. What was my fork? What was I holding on to that I had learned before would give me hope?

3. What was my napkin? Who and what could I count on to catch me?

4. What was the dessert that was coming?

In the case of my mother's death, my empty plate was clearly the one person I loved more than anyone.

My fork was not yet there. Nothing I had learned gave me an understanding of why this would happen. However, that naïve young mind also did not understand the severity or intensity of the loss, so in this case, what I did not know was my guardian angel.

My napkin was my grandmother, my aunt Dottie, and my aunt Sally.

The dessert that would come was the unconditional love from my mother, indelibly marked on the mind of that little seven-year-old for the rest of my life. And let's not forget the beautiful lesson of secrets and what they can eventually reveal.

Some of the most powerful secrets appear out of nowhere, creating unexplainable synchronicities. In my mind, they are gifts handed to us, often in difficult times, as a reminder that life is happening just as it is supposed to.

In the end, all will be okay.

I will explain more about synchronicity in chapter 5, but I'd like to share a powerful incident that happened when I was thirty-five years old. I was on a musical tour that took us around the country, raising money and awareness for AIDS. While in Indianapolis on a cold winter day, I was waiting for others to board the bus and feeling the sadness of everything we had absorbed through meeting so many people in so many cities, all of whom had been affected by the AIDS crisis.

I began to cry, so I got off the bus and strolled through a large city park. Inside a big, open gazebo, I saw a shiny little plaque under the snow. I brushed it off with my gloves. It read: SMILE. LILACS WILL BLOOM HERE IN THE SPRING.

Right there in front of me was my fork, my napkin, and my dessert. Thank you, Mom.

THE MENTAL GYM
Your Auto-Graph

The exercises at the end of each chapter are intended to define the ingredients that constitute your life—past, present, and future. We often sit and reflect on our past or relive moments over and over in our heads. Imagine what might happen if we wrote them down or documented them in the form of a cold, hard graph. What if your life were a corporation? There would be a massive paper trail of charts and graphs, statistics and risk assessments, successes and failures. You would see where mistakes were made and where your company excelled. The board of directors would map a strategic plan based on these documents.

Now it's time to map your strategic plan. Of course, we will account for the main differences between your life and a corporation, which begin with emotions, attitude, and your ability to be motivated by optimism. After all, no progress can be made if you don't have hope. This is a book about hope. Where your mind goes, your energy follows.

By the way, there is no such thing as false hope. That must be the biggest oxymoron in the world, right up there with "terribly pleased," "exact estimate," and "death benefits." If you have hope, you have hope. Period. Looking forward to your future is what brings happiness and optimism, and it all hinges on hope, curiosity, and hard work.

Let's begin to define your future by mapping your past. We'll pretend for a moment that your life was a traded commodity on Wall Street. Instead of a massive paper trail, we will keep it simple by drawing one chart.

Let's have a little fun with your auto-graph.

Draw a simple L-shaped graph. Along the bottom horizontal line, write each year of your life. Up and down the vertical line, place ten equal increments. At the top of the vertical line, write, EXTREMELY HAPPY. At the bottom of that line, write, EXTREMELY SAD. At even intervals going up the line, add the numbers one through ten.

Now, as you go across the graph from left to right, simply put a dot at each year (or every two, three, or five years if it's easier), depicting your level of happiness during that period of your life. Try not to think too much. Allow your emotions and unconscious feelings to quickly determine each dot.

Try to recall key points in your life. What accomplishments make you proud? When did you have the most fun? When were you unemployed or ill? Don't forget births and deaths. Even pets are an important part of happiness. What things brought you the most joy? When were you alone in a good way? When were you alone in a not-so-good way? Other than children or pets, what is your most prized

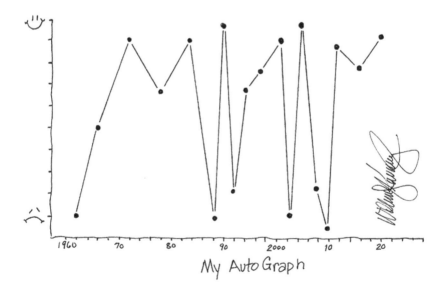

My Auto Graph

possession, and when did you get it? Did you create it? Name something you created that made you proud. Have you mastered a specific skill or talent? What event has dramatically shaped your life? What was a turning point?

Don't forget the times you have been forced to make a change. Include graduations, employment, weddings, having children, deaths, accidents, illnesses, hobbies, crushes, and every other life-changing and life-defining event.

If you have experienced difficulties such as abuse, neglect, or control in your childhood and have not worked through the resulting trauma, I strongly suggest that you seek help from someone who understands and can listen *before* working this graph. When someone has not taken proper and sufficient care to treat a trauma, the consequences often include a strong sense of feeling stuck, or the possibility that a current tragedy might reawaken old trauma. In that case, do not relive it alone. Please find a group or seek individual counseling.

If you are comfortable to continue, you can "connect the dots." Once all the dots have been put on the graph, depicting your life up until now, connect the dots with lines. If you feel compelled, use colors, but don't waste time choosing which ones. Simply pick one and draw.

Suddenly, the graph of your life's journey is right in front of you. This is the path of your new publicly traded corporation. You're ready to sit back, take in its movement and flow, and enjoy it. Is it fairly level? See any extreme highs and lows? The graph will probably surprise you. It might look like a seismograph when an earthquake hits, with extreme highs and lows in a short period of time. Are you surprised where it jumps up or down? Does if often jump way up after it is low, or does it jump way down after it is high? It could be fun to explore the reasons for that.

After you examine the instinctual movement of the graph, think about the circumstances that caused you to mark HAPPY or SAD.

Now it's time to own it, so write your signature across the bottom of your "auto-graph."

We will come back to this graph several times, so complete it now before you read any further. It is a small capsule of your life *as you perceive it*. In ensuing chapters, we will discuss the determining factors for radical changes, both good and bad. What caused them? How did you react? Where did they lead you? Was it good or bad? What made it so?

The wonderful novelist Alice Hoffman says that our lives are made up of equal parts sorrow and joy.[5] Good fortune and bad luck are always tied together with invisible, unbreakable thread, and it is impossible to have one without the other.

WHAT WERE YOUR MOST POWERFUL LIFE MOMENTS?

What were the three best moments and the three most difficult moments of your life? Write three words to describe each of them.
Reflect on each moment. Feel them. It is important not to dismiss these powerful experiences with a simple "Well, that happened."

Pause and reflect.

These moments made you who you are.

Next, focus on the words you wrote to describe these moments. Why did you write each word? What did you learn? What did you accomplish? What changed? What allowed you to thrive because of these moments?

Understanding how these moments create you is the key to thriving, now and in the future. This lesson will become vitally important to you. You have an inner ability to be resilient, and you have the capacity to allow happiness. Now it's time to find out more.

---

5 Alice Hoffman, *Survival Lessons* (Chapel Hill, NC, Workman Publishing, 2013).

A MINDFUL MOMENT

At the end of each chapter, I want to offer suggestions for practicing mindfulness.

Every cell in our body is created with consciousness and energy, not just our brains. All of our physical cells are as busy as our cell phones—times one hundred. Our brains affect the rest of our body, and our body affects our brain. Likewise, everything around us is filled with living cells. A flower begins as a small seed and grows into an energy that affects our senses of sight, smell, touch, sometimes taste, and the consciousness of its beauty. It excites the cells inside us, and it brings peace at the same time. Again, the synchronicity of opposites. Why does a rose have thorns?

A flower offers us so much, but only if we choose to accept. It is known as a symbol of peace and consciousness. "Stop and smell the roses" is just one small example of how everything around us can be transformed into a strong message to stop and simply appreciate this moment. So often, we stress over wanting certain elements of our lives, or the world, to be different. At this moment, these elements are exactly where they are supposed to be, so the stress is a complete waste of brain cells. If you teach yourself to be mindful, to be present, you can change your life.

Research has shown that people who are generally happy and calm usually show more activity in the left side of the brain's frontal area rather than the right side.[6] In contrast, people who tend to be anxious, sad, or stressed often show more activity on the right side of the frontal area. Through concentration, meditation, and mindfulness, activity can be shifted from one side to the other. We can learn to better manage our emotions when we learn to manage our thoughts. Each thought is happening right now, in this moment.

6 Rick Hanson, PhD, *Hardwiring Happiness: The New Brain Science of Contentment, Calm, and Confidence* (New York, NY: Harmony Books, 2013).

Deep inside each of us are many seeds of wisdom, expression, and passion. If we remain constantly busy, we never have the opportunity to discover them. Until we sit quietly, just like a flower or a tree, we can never find those internal elements of true purpose.

To begin our first Mindful Moment, sit comfortably in a chair or on a sofa, either indoors or outside. Place both feet firmly on the ground. Put one hand on your leg and one hand on your stomach. Close your eyes. Take a slow, deep breath for four seconds and feel the air fill your stomach. Hold it for four seconds, and release slowly for four seconds. Repeat three times.

Whatever sounds you hear, let them gently move in one ear and out the other. Hear them and let them go. Concentrate instead on the sensation of your breath. Once you return to your normal breathing, sit quietly with no thoughts. Of course, thoughts will come and go, but allow them to do just that—come . . . and go.

Now move your hand from your stomach up to your heart. Feel the warmth of love, the love you feel for yourself. Slowly focus on the child that is still inside you. Love that child. Concentrate on that child. Take a few minutes to come up with one question that this child wants to ask you. What is something he or she is afraid of? Or what is something he or she is curious about?

Once you have secured that question, contemplate your answer. What is the most powerful one-sentence statement you want this child to know? Perhaps "You have no idea how beautiful your life will become," or "Stay strong. It will pass." Only you can decide what will comfort that child. What is a mantra you might develop to constantly remind yourself of this powerful lesson?

Repeat the line several times. Feel the child as he or she feels it.

Finally, declare to yourself that this will become your mantra, the line you will use throughout other Mindful Moments in this book.

Slowly open your eyes. Look at the sky and say your mantra one more time. Know that it is still true to this day.

CHAPTER 2

Hell in the Hallway

When I was fourteen years old, I was being bullied one day by a group of boys in my class. As I walked outside the main building to go to art class, they all circled me, shoved me back and forth, threw my art supplies on the ground, and called me a loser.

I was a shy, artistic, nonathletic kid, so of course I believed they were right. I was a loser.

After they all ran off, I sat picking up my art supplies, and for a moment, I stopped. I looked up at the sky and said, "This will be the hardest day of my life."

I didn't say this with resignation hopelessness. It was a promise to myself, and I never forgot that statement. Because of the emotions it stills brings to me, I believe it to be true to this day.

Many of us experienced bullying when we were children. Those bullies never had a clue about the gifts they offered us. It was one of our first huge lessons that painful experiences can lead to great achievements—once we stop, feel the hurtful pain, and learn that we are not the losers they called us. Eventually, we can recognize the gifts.

Often adults, not children, are the ones saying this bullying behavior is okay. From the heads of our government to media companies, bullying is a symbol of supremacy and division. We cannot let this define us; we must recognize that this view represents the opposite of progress for equal rights. Every person is human and deserving of dignity.

I know it sounds incredibly Pollyanna-ish to suggest we see the silver lining, but there is a huge one when it comes to bullies. We cannot change them or their thoughts, but we can refocus our own beliefs.

The bullies from my early teens taught me four great life lessons: courage, compassion, addressing shame, and finding hope.

COURAGE

After graduating from high school, I was certainly not afraid to leave that school or small town. Ironically, that courage allowed me to prove to myself that I was not the loser those boys told me I was.

On that day when I told myself it would be the most difficult day of my life, I did not realize that I was really saying, "I have hope that I will never hurt like this again. I have hope that I can be courageous enough to recognize that what others think does not matter. I have hope that I can truly learn what does matter, and always move forward in that direction."

We live in a heteronormative, White-male-dominated culture. Each difficult lesson that made me feel different and alone became another step toward making me unique and my own individual. This bears repeating: our greatest assets and our most cherished gifts come from our most difficult struggles and challenges.

COMPASSION

One step toward empathy for others is to experience our own misfortunes. When we find others who are going through a struggle we have overcome, compassion gives us the ability to be of service, and that is the direct road to happiness. Nothing breaks my heart more than to see a child being bullied. Hopefully he or she will also grow and become a better person because of it, but it does not justify the cruelty or lighten the pain in the moment. I hope a few of them can be as self-aware and melodramatic as I was, embracing the pain and proclaiming how tragic it is to be told we are wrong when we are different.

SHAME

Everyone is different.

Our society promotes shame on so many levels. Whether our struggle relates to weight, disability, finances, family, race, mental problems, or so many other issues, no one is perfect. That imperfection makes us unique and forms our real identity—not the identity society says we "should" have. We learn to internalize shame, which precludes our being proud of who we are. Finding our true identity is the opposite of shame.

Who wants to be perfect? Our imperfections allow us to present our gift to the world. That is the entire point of this book. Brené Brown says that "shame loves perfectionists."[7] If we can't become good at being vulnerable, we become damn good at shame.

My shame was no better or worse than anyone else's. It was based on my sexuality and my artistic traits. Both of those are raw meat for the animals called bullies. Those two "character defects" felt like the exact definition of the words *sissy*, *pussy*, and *faggot*.

Thankfully, I have learned over time that these qualities are the opposite of character defects. They are my gifts. I am a strong believer that artists, performers, writers, and musicians are given deep souls meant to offer emotion and joy to the world. Yet offering that gift requires vulnerability, and it is often rejected or underestimated. Society, particularly in our teen years, does not appreciate sensitivity; it preys on it.

Hopefully we learn that being vulnerable by offering our creative gifts is the path that eventually overpowers shame. When we talk about our feelings or share them through writing, art, or music, we are releasing the shame.

Another step to releasing shame is listening to others. Again,

---

7 Brené Brown, PhD, LMSW, *Gifts of Imperfection; Let Go of Who You Think You're Supposed to Be and Embrace Who You Are* (Center City, MN, Hazelden Publishing, 2020).

compassion. Offer love. Then hear what you are saying to them, and tell yourself the same advice.

In her book *Daring Greatly*, Brené discusses the power of vulnerability in overcoming shame: "Our willingness to own and engage with our vulnerability determines the depth of our courage, and the clarity of our purpose; the level to which we protect ourselves from being vulnerable is a measure of our fear and disconnection."[8]

HOPE

Something at that young age of fourteen told me to just stop, sit down, look up at the sky, and accept the feeling. (Probably because the alternative was to scream and cry.) I have no idea where that guidance came from. It was a surprisingly mindful reaction to sit and recognize my feelings right there, right then.

Fears, tears, and "right heres" are medals of courage.

We can learn to accept the "gift of bullying" by acknowledging the difficulty and then looking for the purpose. We may never find purpose, but we can allow ourselves the exploration.

One thing will always weigh heavily on our excitement about our future: our fear.

Ironically, a portion of our brain loves fear and loss of control. Amusement parks make a lot of money from throwing people into fear and harm's way, and we love it! We pay and wait for hours in line just to be scared. We go to haunted houses to get the adrenaline rush of fear. Just think of all the possible money-makers waiting to be developed. Throwing people in the ocean. Teetering them from the edge of a building. Driving one hundred miles an hour through traffic.

Remember, without fear, we would never accomplish anything

---

8 Brené Brown, PhD, LMSW. *Daring Greatly* (New York, NY: Penguin Random House, 2012).

significant—or develop courage. It is through courage that we discover the reward of excitement. Imagine that reality.

Healthy fear is our friend. It is a major positive element in moving forward. It is *not* an irony that the bigger we dream and the more we want to succeed, the greater our fear. Fear is a disguise for positive change. Change brings new growth.

Fear is a four-letter word, but so is hope.

Then there is the unhealthy fear. The overload of "what-ifs" and what might happen. A woman in one of my groups once said, "I'm worried about the next shoe dropping, even though everything is good right now."

The man sitting next to her said, "Sounds like you don't trust 'good.'"

Hmmm. Trusting good.

When we are cloaked in fear and entrenched in the dark side of sadness, we are unable to see many opportunities. Stepping through and letting go of fear is one of the most difficult challenges we face in life. Playing tug-of-war with our negative emotions seems ridiculous in hindsight, but it can be so very real in the present moment. It might seem that letting go is not an option.

We must allow the emotions that come with fear to exist, not try to brush them aside and ignore them. Dr. Robert Mauer is a professor at UCLA and runs the Science of Excellence consulting firm. He says that we should learn two huge lessons from children: they are not afraid to tell you what they are afraid of, and they do not apologize for crying.[9] When was the last time you heard a small child say, "I'm so sorry that I get emotional when I talk about this"?

We will always have new fears that pop up daily, and then there are the lingering fears we never seem to get rid of.

---

9 Robert Maurer, PhD, *One Small Step Can Change Your Life; The Kaizen Way* (New York, NY: Workman Publishing Co., 2004).

"What you are afraid of is never as bad as what you imagine. The fear you let build up in your mind is worse than the situation that actually exists." —Spencer Johnson, MD

Once we embrace the fear, address it, and step through it, we can search for the light at the end of the fear tunnel.

There are just as many beautiful what-ifs as there are negative what-ifs.

When we are trapped in fear, very often our willpower is not enough to get us out. That is where hope becomes so important. Think of hope as a best friend who sits down next to you and puts its arm around you. You become connected to something outside of yourself. Perhaps hope truly does come from your best friend, or a family member. Welcome the offers of positive connections.

Consider times in your life when you have felt a beautiful presence of hope and profound positivity. Maybe you were looking out at the ocean, or up at the stars, or sitting on a plane and looking at the earth below. Maybe you were listening to music or staring at art. Can you remember the feeling? Hope is not tangible. It is faith. It is trust. It is surrender. It is knowing that everything in the universe has always worked out.

After my incidents of bullying, I became determined not to let the bullies stop me from maintaining my dignity. I strategically became editor of the yearbook, knowing that everyone would be nice to me in order to be flattered in the yearbook. Genius, huh? The only reason I had the courage to run for editor was because of the bullying. I used my skills in art and writing to flip the script and demonstrate how it affects others.

As soon as high school was over—literally the next week—I moved away from that small town. I lied about my age and got a job at an amusement park called Cedar Point, in far northern Ohio on Lake Erie. I lived in the dorms among other workers and was a "ride host" on the Mill Race log flume.

In my freshman year of college, I vividly remember the beginning of our initiation process for my fraternity. I stood on the fireplace hearth with my eighteen fellow pledges while we were harassed by the fraternity members. As they screamed, called us names, and made fun of us, I looked over at the pledge standing next to me. He was a much larger guy who had never been on this side of bullying. He was crying. I remember thinking, *Welcome to my world*. This was nothing in comparison. This was just a fun tradition.

I eventually became vice president, teaming up with my friend Larry, who was president, and my friend Bill, who was treasurer. Both are still good friends to this day. We eliminated hazing during pledging. It worked for about two years, but then it returned by popular demand. Looking back and reflecting on my current beliefs about challenges bringing courage, I can recognize the reason for hazing. I will never condone bullying, but I understand the "manly" reasoning behind trying to make someone stronger through playful ridicule. After all, that mental strengthening was the reason I advanced so much from the bullying. The struggle is the fine line between playful ridicule and dangerous harm.

Even though the bullies on the playground were never aware of the gifts they were giving me, perhaps, just maybe, the fraternity as an organization recognizes the strength and courage that might result. The problem is that most of the individuals doing the bullying are just drunk, naïve young men who are not "bullying for better men."

During that pledging period, I learned the power of "fake courage": alcohol. One night early in my freshman year, I had slightly too much to drink, and I called one of the fraternity leaders an asshole. I was filled with adrenaline-rushing courage, and it was the very first time I had ever felt like "one of the guys." For the first time in my life, I was actually bullying someone else (who needed bullying). It was evil. It was the opposite of human kindness. It was intoxicating!

Everyone laughed, and I realized the power of liquid and chemical fake courage.

When we are younger, courage seems easier. Perhaps that is because of innocence and ignorance, but as we grow older and build comfortable lives, families, and material things, making changes becomes more difficult—indeed, more courageous.

"The awful thing about change is that we want it as much as we fear it and we need it as much as we need safety." —Oprah Winfrey

I had always planned to move somewhere in the South to warmer weather after college; however, the week of my graduation, my father had a heart attack. The following day, when he woke up in the hospital, he asked me why I was still there. "Umm . . . you had a heart attack," I responded. He reached over and handed me the keys to his 1978 Ford Galaxy station wagon, arguably the largest car ever known to mankind.

He told me, "Take my car and go. Risk is nothing more than opportunity disguised as fear."

"But I don't think I should leave you."

Dad took my hand and said, "There will always be reasons to stay, but so many better reasons to move on."

I asked him what I should do when I got there. He said, "Follow your instincts, and trust all that I have tried to teach you. Remember, there is a price for every privilege, and a privilege for every price. Starting tomorrow, I know we will both be getting better."

For the next four nights, I slept in that car. Eventually, after arriving in Dallas, I found an ad in the newspaper for someone looking for a roommate, and the new life began.

Dad unconsciously reminded me of what I had learned from the bullying: to not be afraid to pick up my art supplies and move on.

There was a privilege for that price, and I was excited to take advantage of the courage I had learned.

That quote from my father became a mantra in my life whenever fear stepped in. I repeated that exact quote to him twenty-eight years later on his deathbed. "There will always be reasons to stay, but so many better reasons to move on."

I'm still trusting and following those instincts he instilled in me. It certainly doesn't get easier to take leaps like that as we get older. We accumulate things (and families), and then a lot more things. Moving becomes harder and harder. The older we get, the more we lose when we move forward. Thank God that throughout our lives, we learn strength and endurance. We lose friends, jobs, family, money, dreams, and most of all, the physical strength to help us through it all. Those losses are the education required for courage.

All the more reason to accept the price for the privilege.

There will always be plenty of excuses to not move forward in life. The excuses sound real in our heads: "I can't change jobs because I will lose insurance for my family." "I can't move because it will upset my parents." "I can't relax or take a vacation because there is too much work that needs doing." The sad part is that they are all very real. They are the truth.

As much as we might want to believe it, lack of money is not always what stops us from progressing. Sometimes the abundance of it is to blame—as in "If I make a change, I won't make the same amount of money." Most of us are not willing to alter our external lifestyle to enhance our inner life with satisfaction and fulfillment. Which is more important? Material goods or inner peace and fulfillment? It is a very real decision. How does money affect you? Does it allow you to be who you want to be, or does it cause you to become someone you'd rather not be? That is a difficult and powerful question. It quite honestly might be worth having a terrible job if you have come to appreciate the money. The question is in your "cheese."

In his book *Who Moved My Cheese*, noted physician and children's book author Spencer Johnson states, "The quicker you let go of old cheese, the sooner you will find new cheese."[10] Your cheese is all the old moldy aspects of your life. You might be very attached to your old cheese. Those emotional feelings have so much to do with making a transition.

When we operate from lower emotions like greed, envy, jealousy, fear, and panic, our bodies circulate energy at sluggish, toxicity-producing levels, which don't allow us to grow in consciousness. On the other hand, when we operate from feelings that have a high vibrational charge—emotions such as courage, joy, and compassion—our lives feel blessed and electric.[11]

SELF-COMPASSION

Do not underestimate the vibrational charge of compassion. It begins with you, with self-compassion. That is often our most important first step. There are a lot of myths around the term *self-compassion*. In no way does it mean feeling sorry for yourself, sitting in self-pity and crying. Self-compassion means the opposite. It instigates healing. It leads the transition from bad to good. It can give us courage and strength to move forward by showing ourselves kindness. When we stay stuck in the pity, sadness, and drama, we are not allowing movement to the next step, which is sympathy and change of attitude.

Where might you need comforting? Where might you need forgiveness? Where might you be stuck in past actions that are done and over? Remember that you can sometimes overcome them by using them as motivation for bigger and greater actions.

10 Spencer Johnson, M.D., *Who Moved My Cheese?* (New York, NY: G. P. Putnam's

11 Eva Archer-Smith, www.evaarcchersmith.com. Sons, 1998).

SMALL STEPS

A step forward need only be a small one. Early in my therapy career, I learned that every individual must decide how big the steps should be. We can't compare our progress to others or judge ourselves on the time we might need in order to take those first steps.

As a brand-new intern at the Los Angeles LGBT Center, I was assigned a client who was unemployed and nearly homeless. He was frozen in fear and self-doubt. In one of our sessions, he promised that he would apply for just one job that week. That task proved to be too much, and he remained frozen. The next week he set the goal to simply look at job postings; however, that too was overwhelming.

To me, this seemed so simple: just get on the computer and type in a website. I was at a loss as to how to help him. My supervisor at the time, Susan Holt, wisely suggested that I erase any judgment or expectations and simply ask him if he might be willing to take a smaller step. The next week, he decided that he would simply go to the computer and turn it on with no expectations to do more. Sure enough, he went to his computer, turned it on, went to a website, applied for a job, and got the job, all in a week. Because of his new job, he had no time to see me, and our sessions came to an end. One night, I had a dream that my supervisor and I were sitting in a nest, waving goodbye. We were the proud momma and poppa birds saying farewell to our first baby bird.

That story illustrates the sense of despair that can overcome us. Fear can grow so large that it freezes our ability to take any action at all. We become overwhelmed by negativity, isolated from hope, and begin to feel like there is no way out of our situation. This is a formidable mental condition. Depression sets in, which can lead to anxiety, which leads to more fear.

Remember that each step is progress. Each step, no matter how small, gets easier than the last. Soon they will become giant strides.

Each time we adapt to change allows us to adapt sooner and more productively the next time. Even when mistakes happen along the road, those mistakes come from the courage of stepping further away from the fear. Take pride in those steps! As you move past the fear, you begin to appreciate and feel accomplishment and joy. The answer lies not in finding your goal but in learning to enjoy the search. How can you make it fun?

It's been said several ways by several people, but I have adapted one of my all-time favorite expressions to say "Life is not about the door that will open or the door that closed. It is about enjoying the hell in the hallway."

The next small step might be the wrong step. That's okay. The important part is not the result but the lesson. Life is about learning. Eventually, with work and progress, our fears and our darkness will become what we are most proud of. Our scars are symbols of courage and growth. They represent our passion.

When I was a young boy, I memorized all the lyrics to the song "The Bare Necessities," from Walt Disney's 1967 animated movie *The Jungle Book*. For anyone who knows the song, you will recognize that it is not an easy song to memorize. But still to this day, I can sing, "Don't pick the prickly pear by the paw. When you pick a pear, try to use the claw. But you don't need to use the claw when you pick a pear of the big pawpaw."

The song was nominated that year for an Academy Award for best original song. There's a good reason.

Thirty-five years later, I worked for the Walt Disney Company and helped produce several live shows with that song. It always made me and my coworkers smile as I sang along. However, it wasn't until I was writing this book and I happened to hear the song on the radio that I actually heard and understood the lyrics. At some level, I always knew it was not about "the bear necessities" but "the bare necessities." I just never truly listened to the meaningful advice that is so very vital to the core of this book. *The Jungle Book*'s audience is far too young to understand the importance of those lyrics. I sang it for years simply for the fun, upbeat music—and, of course, Baloo's laughter throughout the song.

Look for what is important, and focus on the beauty around you. Be happy, and the necessities of life will come to you. Don't work too hard, and don't spend your time looking for something that can't be found. Every line is such a gem.

"Old Mother Nature's recipes" is a beautiful metaphor for life's difficult plans. Each downturn is simply part of the recipe for our lives. But the bees will still be buzzing in the trees. And why? To make honey for you and me. And "when you look under the rocks and plants, take a glance at the fancy ants. The bare necessities of life will come to you."[12]

DIRT, DREAMS, AND DIRTY DREAMS

We often hear the terrible insult of something or someone being "dirt." Let's look at dirt. It lies there, doing no one wrong. It never gossips or tells lies. It gets walked on by everyone.

And yet:

It births food for the world. It gives us the beauty of flowers and trees. It is one of the most unattractive materials on earth, and yet it gives completely of itself to yield our most beautiful and essential life elements.

It's where the lilacs grow . . . as well as all of the secrets and blessings that come with them.

Dirt is actually not unattractive. Several years ago, I started collecting dirt. Yes, you read that correctly. I began the collection while driving across the country and seeing the amazing changes of color in

---

12 Music and Lyrics by Terry Gilkyson, Sung by Phil Harris, The Walt Disney Company, all rights reserved.

different soils. I thought it would be fun to collect dirt from famous landmarks around the world. Eventually, I had a beautiful display of small bottles of dirt from dozens of countries and famous locations. Even my grandmother (illegally) brought me dirt from Christ's tomb, along with a very funny photo of her sneaking it into her purse.

A few years later, a friend in Boston decided he wanted to take my collection a step further, and he started a "dirt museum." I sent him all of my samples, except for a few very personal ones, like Grandma's.

The moral of this little story? Nothing is "just" dirt. Dirt can be fascinating. What some might call "just dirt," others see as a beautiful element worthy of a museum.

Everything can become a treasure with a little thought and creativity. Once again, what we perceive as dull, sad, or a curse can transform into a butterfly. That first time I stopped in Oklahoma to scoop up a little yellow dirt, I would have *never* dreamed it would be the beginning of a dirt museum in Boston. That little yellow bottle now sits in a frame in the reception area.

I once met a young man at the *Fast Company* magazine convention who had started a corporation that earned millions of dollars. He made fertilizer out of worm poop. Yes, he literally made a fortune from nothing but shit. And he took it many steps further. All of his packaging containers were pre-used soda bottles. His company paid five cents to schools for collecting and recycling each plastic bottle. It was a win-win for everyone. Even the worms got fed well. It is the perfect example of literally turning shit into opportunity.

Someone somewhere came up with the idea to take water, normal water from a spring, put it in bottles, and sell it. We are essentially just buying the bottles. It works. Billions of dollars are spent on plain old bottled water. We've been brainwashed to believe we must drink healthier water. A good friend of mine says he used to snort cocaine off toilet seats but would *never* drink tap water.

Who is old enough to remember pet rocks? Someone had the bright idea to take rocks—yes, rocks—and sell them as pets. People bought them! They bought a rock they could have grabbed from their yards. They also bought the entire concept of making it a pet.

Dirt, shit, rocks, and water. All free if we choose. Yet they are the perfect example of taking absolutely nothing and creating an exciting and arguably rewarding product by simply twisting perspective.

This concept can be carried so much further as motivation to rethink our misfortunes. Simply rewire your perspective.

Two people in one of my support groups disclosed that they both suffer from bipolar disorder. Both were artists. The first gentleman felt that he had been cursed with bipolar disorder his entire life and it negatively affected his creativity. The other artist, a young woman, explained that she did not think of it as a curse but rather a blessing. When she is working on her paintings, she believes her brain is on fire. But it tells her when to slow down, take a break, and be at peace.

Similarly, when we feel that we are stuck in our lives and nothing is going right, we can redirect that massive train and recognize that with all the valuable cargo we are hauling, we can choose to set the tracks in a new direction. We might not yet know the destination, but we can redirect the train.

If I said it was simple, I would be lying. The train can be huge, and the challenge daunting.

The moral of all of this is that when you are given lemons, don't make something as boring as lemonade. Make something ingenious and uniquely you. A lemon museum? A lemon skincare product? A million lemon pets to sell to the world? Just stare at a lemon and think of what you might do with it. That is a perfect metaphor for looking at your life.

In the opening, I explained the four metaphorical stages of holding on to your fork. In this case of my bullying experience at the age of fourteen, here is how I answer the questions raised by those stages:

1. What was my empty plate? In other words, what was taken away from me? In this case, it was every ounce of dignity. I was being told I was worthless, and I believed it.

2. What was my fork? What was I holding on to that I had learned would give me hope? At that age, I'm not sure I had a fork, but because I literally picked up my art supplies, I'll say that I hoped that with my artistic talent, I could someday use that experience to express myself. Most amazing to me is that I stood up and said that no day in my life would be harder. So I clearly had hope that life could only get better. I was confident that I would someday leave that small town and become a much stronger person.

3. What was my napkin? Who and what could I count on to catch me? That question was what troubled me the most. I could not go to my father and admit that I was bullied. I was lost as to finding someone to whom I could admit my shame. My napkin was not yet there, or it was as yet undiscovered.

4. What was the dessert that was coming? My dessert was enormous. It would grow to be a life of courage, accomplishments, and an ability to prove that I was not a loser.

After moving to Dallas, I immediately took a job as a room-service waiter at the Marriott Hotel. Just one more great book of stories. Within three months, I was hired by the Freeman Companies as a graphic designer for live entertainment events. This time, no one threw my art supplies at me and called me a loser. Instead, they promoted me to art director and eventually director of production and moved me to Houston. Yet another new beginning.

Thank you, Dad.

"Risk is nothing more than opportunity disguised as fear. There will always be reasons to stay, but better reasons to move on."

THE MENTAL GYM
Explore Old Photographs

What photos show the key moments of your life? Exploring your old photographs can be a great way to identify your most impactful moments. In therapy, photo analysis is a powerful tool for exploration. Once you know what to look for, photos can be more telling than you ever knew. Who is sitting next to whom? Who is smiling? Who is touching others? Who is not touching? Who might be standing alone? Who looks scared? Who is looking at whom? What is his/her expression? Do the faces in the photo reflect the personalities you remember?

Perhaps categorize your photographs into three groups: the happiest moments, the saddest moments, and the most powerful moments. Maybe happy to sad. Maybe chronologically. Perhaps in order of importance. Arrange the photos on the wall in whatever categories you choose.

Not to sound morbid, but what photos would you want displayed at your funeral? Put them in a certain box as your favorite photos.

Once you discover an old photo of yourself at an age four through ten, sit and concentrate on that photo. Write a letter to that child. What do you want to say? Remember your mantra from the first Mental Gym.

A MINDFUL MOMENT

For your second Mindful Moment, find a quiet, comfortable, and private space outside. Allow yourself to lie quietly for a few minutes, either on the grass, the sand, or on a lounge chair. Place your hands on your stomach, or lay them along your sides.

Begin again with deep breaths, into the stomach. Hold each breath for four seconds before releasing for a count of four. Let yourself become completely relaxed. Be aware of the contact between your body and the surface it is on. Feel the heaviness and the weight pressing down. Feel the temperature, the breeze, and the air. What do you smell?

Keep your eyes open and focus on the sky above. Watch the clouds pass over. If it's nighttime, stare at the stars. This is a beautiful exercise at night. You have listed the most powerful moments. Let each one be represented by a cloud or a star. Focus on them, each one symbolizing a struggle or a beautiful moment.

Allow the sun or the moon to be your shining light of hope. Focus on the strength and courage it represents to you.

Take several deep breaths throughout this mindfulness exercise, and allow yourself to drift away into your past. Repeat your mantra from chapter 1's Mindful Moment.

CHAPTER 3

If You're Handing Us That Lemon, You Better Expect Something Fabulous

E verything about our lives, our attitude, and our happiness, is about perspective. We are all completely different in how we view the world as it happens to us. Some look at the glass as half full, others as half empty. Still others look at the glass and wonder how it was possibly created, or marvel at the reflecting colors—or a chosen few might wonder when in the hell you are going to drink it!

We all have immediate responses to life's changes, particularly in a tragedy. However, as we heal, we can begin to change perspective. How might I grow from this? How might I change and help myself, and how might I help others?

In one of my addiction recovery groups, a twenty-year-old woman was talking about her favorite Bruno Mars songs. Because one of them was "Locked Out of Heaven," I asked her if she felt she was locked out of heaven because she couldn't drink with her friends. Her response showed a completely different perspective than I was anticipating. She said, "I have been sober just long enough to recognize that I have found the key to the lock and I can now enter heaven." There was not a dry eye in the room.

Another example of perspective is the manner in which LGBTQ people begin to identify with their true selves. Like all of life's internal struggles, sexuality is difficult to accept personally. That road to acceptance includes talking to others. It has always been referred to as "coming out." Why not take an entirely different creative perspective and "invite them in"? That is the basis of "gay pride." To have the perspective to appreciate self-identity and see such a deep, personal disclosure as a gift to the people you tell, particularly those you choose as the first to know, is a blessing. You're saying, "I am letting you into my life" rather than "I am telling you something that is shameful and you don't want to hear."

In any difficult situation, we should take the point of view that we are offering the gift of trusting someone enough to share our deepest feelings. It is often a beautiful beginning to a conversation to say, "I love you so much that I want you to be the person I can talk with."

When life gives you that lemon, hold it with someone and embrace it. Don't worry about the lemonade yet. That's further down the road. For now, just feel, smell, and taste the lemon. In the beginning, it might be more than a little sour.

My move to Houston was life changing on many levels. I advanced rapidly and unexpectedly in my career, and I was still struggling with my sexuality. I moved into a large apartment complex and met a few of my neighbors, who were a strong impetus in edging me in the correct direction—toward the door out of the closet.

It is not a cliché that gay men struggle with accepting themselves far more than others struggle to accept them. For me, my biggest thought was that I would be proving the bullies right. All of that harassment taught us that "sissy" and "faggot" were the worst things a human could possibly become.

One of the worst possible consequences was the disappointment I would cause my father. As I mentioned, he was a basketball player and a soldier. He had hopes that his two sons would follow in his footsteps, not that I would skip way down the yellow brick road. I owed him my life and everything I had been given. He didn't deserve to be disappointed. I was disappointing him.

I know now that there is no such thing as "choosing to be gay." Never in a million years would I have "chosen" to be gay. I would have done anything in the world to not be "one of them." It's difficult to brush aside everything you have ever learned and decide to accept yourself for who you were truly meant to be. Telling everyone who has loved you for your entire life that their beliefs about you are wrong is traumatic. So I didn't. Why cause confrontation? Just live a secret life, move as far away as possible, and pretend.

I had to begin by mourning the loss of who I had hoped to be. Back then, if you were gay, there was no chance of having children or even a big wedding. Anyone I loved would have to be a secret. Or worse, I would be alone my entire life. The shame was overwhelming.

Becoming proud of who I am was a long process. Eventually, just like every challenge in my life, it became a huge blessing. So many of my greatest accomplishments and joys have come from skipping down that yellow brick road. Just like Dorothy, I found some great friends, learned true courage, and found my heart. I've had a life in living color—and certainly witnessed a few flying monkeys.

The first person in my family who I finally decided to tell I was gay was my sister Kathy. She was coming to visit me in Houston, and I spent a lot of time planning just how I was going to tell her. I decided that soon after she arrived, I would get it over with quickly by taking her to a nice restaurant and telling her how much I loved my family, how much I had struggled with discovering myself, and giving an entire long lecture about who I had become.

Soon after we sat down in the restaurant, I was handing her a cup of coffee. My hand was shaking so hard that Kathy looked me in the eyes and said, "If you don't hurry up and tell me you're gay, we're both going to have coffee spilled all over us."

My whole speech went out the window. She knew. She cared. And she loved me.

My four fork categories?

1. What was my empty plate? What was taken away from me?
   It was my belief that I could simply be like any other strong

man: I could get married, have children, and be a "normal" member of society. That was never going to happen.

2. What was my fork? What had I learned before that would give me hope? I learned from the bullies that they were wrong. I could be whoever I was meant to be . . . and still be a "normal" member of society.

3. What was my napkin? Who and what could I count on to catch me? I knew that there were people in my life I could count on to love me no matter what. Because I loved them so much, I didn't want to hurt them, so, ironically, they were the most difficult to tell.

4. What was the dessert that was coming? There are no words to express the joy that would become my life. I learned that being gay means celebrating every step of joy. This is the first story to prove that:

As I became more comfortable in the gay community, I dated a few men. One day at work, we were all moving furniture. I shouted to everyone, "I'll get the love seat by myself." My coworker Nancy shouted back, "You always do!"

Then she sat me down on it and said she was going to give me an assignment. I had told her that I felt lonely going into the Thanksgiving weekend. She told me to go to a gay bar on Thanksgiving day and look for the nicest person in there. "He doesn't have to be the most beautiful. Simply the kindest-looking man."

I followed her assignment. After looking around the bar, I spotted exactly the person she had suggested. He was handsome *and* he looked like a very good human being. I walked up to him and said, "You look like the nicest person in here." He stared at me for a few seconds and then said, "Wow. You really don't know how to play the game, do you?"

Within one month, we owned a home together.

Randy was truly kind from his core. He was also accomplished in business and a great family man to his mother and sister. Everyone loved him.

As I mentioned, I had not told my father about my personal life. He knew I bought a house with another man, and I assumed he probably had a clue. When Dad's second wife died, I invited him to come to Houston to stay with us for Thanksgiving, knowing he would never say yes because he had not been on a plane since World War II.

He said yes.

Randy's mother was also going to be staying with us. She had buried two husbands, so they had a lot in common . . . . except that she was a staunch Republican and he was a staunch Democrat. Oh well. We'd just see how this went.

Other than the day I met Randy, it was truly the best Thanksgiving of my life. Randy's mother and my father hit it off instantly. They took walks together (we were not allowed to join them), and they laughed themselves silly making political jokes about each other. I remember my dad saying, "Since you're from North Carolina, you must be so proud of Jimmy Carter." In her very strong Southern accent, she replied, "Lordy, Lordy. For four years I couldn't tell anyone where I was from."

I turned to Randy and said, "If these two get married and move in with us, I get the rights to the TV show."

I also knew that Randy and my father would get along. I didn't need to make any introductions in advance because I knew how similar they were. I guess it's true that we marry our parents. Both of them were strong, independent men, and both were in real estate. Right off the bat, they would have a lot to talk about.

Despite that beautiful weekend, Dad never mentioned anything about Randy and me being a couple. It was left unsaid. However, a few years later, he showed me quietly how much he loved me.

As I will explain later, Randy became very ill with AIDS. He told me that before he died, he wanted to visit my father, just as Dad had done for him. He also wanted to see where I grew up. It was on his bucket list, but it was very much on my fuck-it list. I was not excited about staying together at my father's home.

We went one cold winter weekend, and as we walked up the driveway, Randy asked me if I was uncomfortable. I said, "Let the AIDS parade begin."

As he opened the door, the very first thing out of Dad's mouth was, "Do you boys want separate rooms, or do you want to sleep together?"

Oh. Dear. Baby. Jesus.

I knew he had probably rehearsed that question many times in his head and just needed to get it out there. I was proud of him. He was stepping out of his comfort zone and trying to be a loving father. But what happened that night was the crowning jewel of his acceptance.

Randy was not feeling well after the long trip and the cold weather. He fell asleep on the sofa in the living room after dinner while Dad cleaned the kitchen. I went upstairs to get something from my suitcase, and as I was coming down the stairs, unbeknownst to Dad, I saw him put a blanket over Randy and kiss him on the forehead while he was sleeping.

That moment will forever be one of the most beautiful in my life. Dad loved me. He just was not comfortable saying it.

"THE AIDS" AND THE '80S

Like most people, each decade of my life has had challenges and subsequent rewards. The 1980s were no exception. Early in that decade, a couple of my friends became very ill. It was soon evident that they had developed the new "gay cancer," which later became known as GRID, gay-related immune disease. Eventually it was called AIDS. The appetizer was called HIV. And to all the well-meaning outsiders, it was often called "the AIDS."

There was no test. There was no cure. There was no knowledge regarding the disease in the medical industry.

It had been a struggle to overcome the shame of being gay. Now we had to overcome a new shame of bringing a deadly disease to the world. Suddenly there was no hiding our gay lives. This disease brought us all out under a spotlight. In the beginning, it was the worst thing that could happen. We now had shame on shame, and both were being exposed. Eventually we recognized that instead of hate, there was also much love and compassion. Not only were people accepting us, but they also wanted to help us through the journey.

We were all frightened. Others became frightened of us too. No one knew anything about how the disease was transmitted or how long it took to see symptoms. There were beliefs that if you kissed a gay person, you might get AIDS. Or even if you touched them. On one of my visits to the dentist, they completely wrapped my body in cellophane. They did it while laughing and telling me that I was so special they wanted to preserve me, but I knew what they were doing.

One by one, the closest people in my life began to die.

Kevin was the first gay man I had ever met, at the pool at my apartment complex when I first moved to Houston. He introduced me to a group of men who would become my closest friends. All but one of them died.

Brad was the first man I truly loved. I had broken up with him because I loved him too much. As unbelievable as that sounds, it is the truth. A few weeks ago, I was telling a friend about Brad and the love I still felt for him. The next morning, I got a call from an elderly woman in Arkansas. I almost didn't take the call because I had no idea who it was. It was Brad's mother. I couldn't believe she'd found me. She wanted me to know that it had been thirty-five years since his death. "He loved you, darlin'." I hung up in total shock, and then I sobbed, reliving those tragic days, processing her words, embracing his love, and trying to absorb the incredible synchronicity of having just talked about Brad the night before.

Ronnie was one of my closest friends. He struggled so much on his deathbed, crying for hours, saying that he didn't want to leave us.

Wally worked for me at the production company. He was also a model. His partner *Duane* was an ex-partner of Randy. All three of them died a few months apart from each other.

Pat was a beautiful man whose heart I had once broken. While he was in the hospital for his final week, I took him a large painting I had created of a night we dressed up for Halloween. He turned his head away and said he couldn't look at it. It hurt too much. "Please take it away," he cried.

There were so many others, but one of the most painful deaths was *Mark's*.

In late 1991, I was walking down the hallway of the hospital, visiting a friend. I glanced in a room and saw a young man I had briefly known, named Mark. He was lying quietly with his eyes closed and a tear running down his cheek.

I walked in the room and asked him if he remembered me. He did. He explained to me that the doctors had told him that morning that he had little time left. He had moved to the city recently and hadn't made any close friends. His parents had disowned him because he was gay. He was all alone.

I asked Mark if he had any thoughts about what was next on his journey. Was he spiritual, or did he believe in an afterlife? His response was profound.

"I just want to die and be forgotten."

Because of the intense sadness of that statement, I remember him the most. That response burned into my heart. No one should have to die alone. No one should die with that level of shame. Mark is one more soul for whom I write this book.

There was another friend who did not die of AIDS but whose

sad loss came around the same time. *Richard* and I were exactly alike. We met in a professional situation while I was producing a show for his sister Kathy. Kathy was the owner of the advertising agency, I was the producer, and Richard was the graphic designer for the show. He and I were the same age and both had degrees in graphic design. The only difference: he was a much better designer than I was.

Richard and I had other similarities. We were both in our late twenties and struggling with our sexuality. Neither one of us talked about it, but when we were together, there was extreme tension due to our confusion, challenged even more by an attraction for each other. Neither of us had the courage to say anything.

Kathy and I had worked together on previous projects and became friends; however, this was my first time working with Richard. The show was a huge success. The clients were very happy.

Shortly after the show, Kathy and Richard were walking on the beach, and he revealed his secret to her. He told her that he was gay. She was shocked and sad. As do most family members, Kathy worried about him. She loved him and she feared that this might lead to a life of unhappiness as he could by shamed by society. This was the early 1980s. She explained her sadness to him.

That evening, Richard took his life.

Kathy and I became even closer. She dedicated her life to helping the gay community in Richard's honor. It was the very beginning of the AIDS crisis, and she produced many fundraisers and marketing materials. No one worked as hard as Kathy in her apology to Richard. One day in the 1990s, I told her that she had done enough. Richard was proud.

Richard is one more person helping me write this book. His story could have been mine. As I just mentioned, I have a sister Kathy who I love dearly and who was also the first person I told I was gay. The outcome could have been different. But I move forward with Richard's spirit guiding me, as his sister taught me, to bring purpose and beauty to his tragic ending.

This morning, as I was writing this, Richard's sister texted me and asked how my life is going.

FINDING SOUL IN SADNESS

Difficulties in our lives will challenge our faith. The reality is that those difficulties can strengthen it, but we have to truly contemplate and make every attempt to find the positive forces of our soul, or our spirituality, whatever they might be. Mark did not have time to find that last stage of acceptance. At the young age of twenty-three, he never had the chance to find hope.

The definition of faith in the dictionary is "trust." Faith does not have to be religious. A level of trust will give us hope. Hope will give us motivation for the pursuit of happiness.

While I watched so many friends suffer and waste away from AIDS, I witnessed a new kind of love and support. Priorities became clear, death became real, and generosity from all around the world became profound. That was one enormous blessing hidden in the crisis we were all experiencing: everyone bonded together in a humbling and beautiful way. We began raising money to care for the men who could not afford food or medical treatment We raised money to pay for funerals, for research, for housing, and for monuments. We had to do something to convert our exploding emotions into action. If you hand a tragedy to gay men, you better expect it to eventually be perfectly wrapped with a shining glitter bow like no one has ever seen.

The response was overwhelming. Still to this day, I am moved by the number of people who stepped up to help us. One of the fundraisers I chaired in Houston raised more money than any fundraiser in that city's history. A huge part of that is attributable to Ken Lay, the founder, CEO, and chairman of Enron. Although he was later convicted of criminal actions, he was a kind and generous man and an enormous part of raising money for our cause.

People all around the country began creating unique fundraisers. Indeed, the AIDS crisis taught the world how to put the *fun* in fundraiser. We began walks, runs, and rides. (I always wanted to start a "crawl," but to this day I can't find anyone willing to take that risk.) We put on shows like no one had seen before. Many of them are still happening as annual events.

Then came the brilliant idea for everyone to make beautiful quilts in what became the national Names Project AIDS Memorial Quilt. Transferring sorrow into hours making quilts was a positive method of healing for me and thousands of others. It was a genius idea for many reasons. Each panel is three by six feet, the size of an average grave. They are handcrafted from every country around the world. The panels currently memorialize more than 94,000 people. It was displayed on the National Monument in Washington, DC, in 1987 and then again in 1996. For the second display, I was fortunate enough to be one of the speakers, just behind Lilly Tomlin, to read the names of those memorialized.

I was also honored to be a part of a nationally touring production called *Heart Strings*. I am not sure I will ever have a more profound and spectacular year than 1989. I witnessed the tragedies of thousands of lives lost, and I made the best friends of my life, many of whom are still close friends. We traveled to almost every major city, and for each production we had A-list celebrities, local choirs, and audiences of thousands.

Thanks to David Sheppard, the amazing creator of *Heart Strings*, I was able to play a small part in that beautiful production of music, staging, costumes, and love. We were singing and dancing smack in the middle of an epidemic. That is the lesson of this book. No matter what, some people will always dance. And hopefully that energy will spread.

On opening night during our New York performance, a young

man came backstage and told us he had a big idea. He had created little red ribbons for all of us to wear on our lapels. My first thought was, *Oh, God love ya, honey,* but Christopher Reeves (the original Superman), one of our hosts that night, said he would definitely wear it, so the rest of us followed his lead. I still have that little ribbon.

That simple idea became a symbol for fundraisers around the world. There are now pink ribbons, blue ribbons, yellow ribbons, and several other colors.

One other memorable story from *Heart Strings* occurred during our show in San Diego where Michelle Pfeiffer agreed to be one of our hosts. The night of the show just happened to be the day after she won a Golden Globe for *The Fabulous Baker Boys.* Because of that, she asked me not to have any press backstage to interview her. I agreed; however, I didn't tell her that *Entertainment Tonight* was going to be in the theater. Of course, they managed to get to her, and she was not happy. After the show, she threw her hotel key at me and said she was driving back to Los Angeles.

I was very apologetic, but then I realized I could take her suite at the hotel. When I arrived, I noticed that she had left the bathtub full, with the soap bubbles still flowing over the top. I immediately ran to the store and bought several water bottles, emptied them out, and filled them with water from the tub. Eventually, I had new labels made for the bottles that read, Pfizzy Pfiesty Pfeiffer, and I gave them as Christmas gifts to my brothers-in-law and other straight male friends who always proclaimed that they would drink her bath water.

That epidemic allowed the gay community to explode with passionate talent. If you give a disease to a group of creative performance artists, get ready for a fantastic show. A perfect example of that was all the beautiful funerals and celebrations of life we held for so many. Those elaborate and inspiring days were exact representations of balancing forced and sad goodbyes with the beautiful new beginnings.

One of the funerals I remember most was for a friend who had been a member of the Houston Opera, the Gay Men's Chorus, and his church choir. Somehow, the funeral "event team" was allowed to shut down Main Street, and just as the funeral began, the entire opera, chorus, and choir came marching down the street in matching robes, singing a tribute to him. The gentleman standing next to me whispered, "He wins." He was right. It had become a funeral competition. When handed lemons, gays make extravagant yellow parade floats with rose-petal sculptures and confetti-blasting cannons.

HIS FINAL STRUGGLE

In 1985, they finally came out with a test for the virus. Most people I knew did not want to get tested because there was no treatment and they did not want to deal with the fear of knowing.

My partner Randy and I decided it was the right thing to do. We both tested positive, and the doctor told us to "get our affairs in order" because we probably had about five years to live. Within a year, that doctor died, and our next primary doctor died.

Randy's health began to decline around 1987. Early in 1988, he was too sick to keep his job as an executive for a major title company. He always claimed that losing his job was ten times harder than the diagnosis. He felt that being stripped of his purpose was the worst curse he could be handed, and yet, just two years later, he said that he finally recognized that losing his purpose was the stepping stone to finding his true purpose. Indeed, he kept his fork, and something sweet was delivered to him. He wrote in his journal almost daily, with the emphatic request that I not read a single word until after his death.

Simultaneously in 1988, there was a lottery in Houston for the first medication trial for AIDS, called AZT. Thousands of people signed up for the trial, but only one hundred men would be allowed to join the study. Randy was one of the winners of the lottery.

The trial began with twenty-four pills per day. Within a year, most of the men had died because of the amount of medication being prescribed to them. Randy suspected he was taking too many pills, telling me that he felt his body was being poisoned. So he took twelve, he gave me four, and he gave the rest to other desperate friends. Eventually, after the trials were over, the authorized prescribed dosage was four pills per day. To this day, I believe Randy saved my life by sneaking me those pills. I remember when my doctor excitedly prescribed me AZT, I said, "Oh, don't worry. I've been taking it for a year."

However, even the twelve daily pills Randy took eventually claimed his life. Watching this handsome forty-one-year-old man deteriorate into the appearance of a ninety-year-old was difficult. One night, we were sitting in a restaurant, and he saw a man with AIDS walk in. He whispered to me, "If I ever start to look that old, please let me die." He had no clue that he already looked much older than that man. It made me cry, and yet I couldn't tell him why.

I remember one incident most clearly about our journey with his health. We were lying in bed one night, watching *Seinfeld*, and Randy could not stop coughing. I reached a breaking point. Lost in a sea of anger and fear, I got up from the bed and said, "I will come back when you stop coughing." As I walked to the kitchen, I felt like this was the cruelest thing I had ever done to anyone, and yet I kept begging myself for forgiveness. I was spinning in a whirlwind of frustration and pounding passion to understand myself. I got to the kitchen and started sobbing.

Randy and I always called each other Pokey and Gumby. He came to the kitchen, hugged me, and said, "I'm so sorry, Pokey, that I am ruining your life."

Ruining my life.

Nothing could have been further from the truth.

There were no words. His beautiful soul continuously demonstrated the power of living a genuine and authentic life, not ruining life. That was my confused frustration. We lived in constant fear, but beneath that fear were lessons and growth that can only be planted by challenge, love, courage, and the confrontation of death. To this day, I believe that the purpose Randy was struggling to find became a directive in helping me find my own purpose. I know it is never truly discovered. I always ask him for direction.

We had many beautiful conversations about the afterlife and his potential abilities to communicate with me from the other side. I asked him what signs would let me know he was with me. He said, "You won't need a sign. You'll just know." I responded, "Okay, but just so I know, give me a sign." We agreed it would be whenever I found a penny.

Randy was correct. I don't need a sign. There have been a few distinct incidents when there was not a doubt in my mind he was there to help me. That said, every time I see a penny, I say a little prayer and say, "Thank you, Gumby." It brings such warmth and peace to my heart. I "trust" that his spirit and all that he taught me are buried deep in my heart. Just like my mother, Randy will always be there in me. All I have to do is listen.

As he lay in his hospital bed in January 1992, just ten days before his forty-third birthday, Randy was in and out of consciousness. I was holding one hand, and his mother was holding his other hand. I looked up at her and said, "Thank you for giving us this beautiful man." She didn't stop staring at him as she responded, "I didn't do anything. I just had the extraordinary blessing of being his mother." He quietly whispered, "I love you," moved his fingers to wave goodbye, and took his last breath.

MY EMPTY PLATE. MY FORK.
MY NAPKIN. MY DESSERT.

1. What was my empty plate? In other words, what was taken away from me? Life as I knew it. It seemed as though everything and everyone I loved was gone. I felt empty, but at

the same time, I felt motivated and inspired to find meaning in the darkness.

2. What was my fork? What was I holding on to that I had learned would give me hope? I learned from this experience that I had a purpose. I may never quite discover why I was selected to live, but my purpose is to continually search and explore.

4. What was my napkin? Who and what could I count on to catch me? I discovered an entire community of people who wanted to help those affected by AIDS. As I mentioned, the beauty of that period was the love and compassion that came from so many directions.

5. What was the dessert that was coming? I didn't realize it at the time, but the emptiness prompted by all the deaths would send me away from Houston and into a brand-new, enormous life.

BEGINNINGS AND ENDS

I began this book with a metaphor about a baby coming into this world. This book is about life. That means a beginning and an end.

It seems nonsensical that I would talk about death in a book about hope and optimism. That is exactly why I am doing it. We have a terrible stigma in our society that birth is to be celebrated but death is to be dreaded. We "give" birth, but we can only "accept" death. They are both natural and inevitable. Why not allow your thoughts on death to be positive and optimistic? Not unlike puberty, it might be a lot more fun on the other side.

There are so many questions to consider in thinking about the end. Allow yourself to enjoy the process of thinking about them. These are aside from the typical end-of-life paperwork that can be sad, such as turning off life support, pain, where to be buried, etc.

Think about the other types of questions:

- Who do I want with me at the time of my death?
- Who do I *not* want with me?
- What would I like to be wearing?
- What would I like said at my memorial?
- Do I want a memorial?
- What words do I want used to describe my life?

Reverend Olivia Rosemarie Bareham is a certified death midwife. That's right. She assists families in the process and discusses home deaths and home funerals. Within that discussion is a history of the formation of the funeral home business. I come from a family of funeral directors, and I think Olivia would agree that the very word *directors* emphasizes her philosophy.

She explained that the industry became so powerful in the early 1930s that they convinced *Lady's Home Journal* to coin the phrase *living room* instead of parlor so that it would not be considered a place to die but rather a place for living. In turn, the funeral "homes" took the word *parlor*. People still had their bodies displayed in the parlor; it was just no longer in their homes. It was in another "home" that you had to pay for.[13]

Death is so much more than a living room, a parlor, or directives. When discussing birth, we don't talk about the room, the doctor, or the legal rights of the parents. We tear up with joy for the mother and father. We fantasize about all the miracles that will happen for the future of this human being. Of course, at death we are saying goodbye, and that is extremely difficult, but every goodbye means a new hello. We can cherish the millions of beautiful moments this person has experienced. We can look back and see miracles that at their birth had never been dreamed of.

---

13 Olivia Rosemarie Bareham, Rev, *Sacred Crossings* (Los Angeles, CA). www.sacredcross-ings.com.

There is an honor to being present for someone's last breath. Just like at birth, you are witnessing the process of life.

THE LOSS OF OUR ASSUMED FUTURE

A new insight and awareness came from the confrontation with sudden illness. I quickly learned that nothing is permanent. Anything can happen suddenly, good or bad. We went from drinking and dancing to death and dying.

To deal with that uncertainty and fear in 1990, I took classes in grief from a wonderful instructor and author named Elizabeth Harper Neeld. I learned that often the element of life we must learn to grieve the most is *the loss of our assumed future*. I will continue to reference this concept because it is such a vital step to healing.

Grieving is a necessary process following any tragedy. That is why when I talk about my definition of positive thinking, I am not making light of serious setbacks or in any way suggesting that we just need to "get over it" and think happy. Positive thinking is only one element in our healing.

Grief, however, in its process is not negative. It's pure and healthy and a natural human transition as it leads us through to a level of acceptance. There is nothing to fear about it, because it can also be described as an awareness of love. Crying is a strong part of it. Whether we're crying over a death, a fear, an accident, or a loss, love is the basis of it.

Ever since that epidemic, I have asked myself every day, "Why me?" Why did I survive when so many talented, compassionate, intelligent, and beautiful people did not? What am I meant to do in their honor? I continue to ask them, "What do you want me to do for you today?"

What began as "survivor's guilt" transformed into "survivor's motivation." I can live every day exploring the question of why and then hopefully answer it through my actions. Sometimes they ask too much, and I have to take a break. I forget to ask them what I can do for myself. If there is anything I have learned in my training with family members of cancer patients, it is that self-care is not selfish. Self-care is vital in order to help anyone else. Remember the oxygen mask mandate.

During the display of the Names Project AIDS Memorial Quilt in 1994, I took a photo of Randy's quilt. Several colorful maple leaves from the nearby trees had blown across it. I titled the photo *Fallen Leaves and Risen Souls*.

The quilts and the leaves were both beautiful displays of death and color. Combined, they were symbols of hope, beauty, and eternity, the three basic messages of Randy's journal.

From that photo, I created a series of paintings. Each one showed a personal possession of Randy's, such as cuff links, accomplishment pins, or tie clips, and a quote from his journal. As I mentioned, I had promised not to read his journal until after his death. It was about as profound as anything I have ever done when I came home from his funeral, pulled it out of the dresser drawer, and held it for several minutes before putting it away. It was too difficult.

Eventually, I was able to not only read it but also choose some of the most beautiful quotes from it and publish a book titled *I Know the Time Is Now*, which is how his journal began.

Here are just a few of the quotes:

"As I write this in preparation for my transition into the next phase of existence, I have an overwhelming gratitude for the love and lessons each of you has helped me learn. I look back and remember periods in my life that seemed boring, unpleasant and tediously long, but yet I now realize as this earth life comes to a close that these various times were but a dot in time. It is helpful to remember that things pass with time. What a blessing that is in so many ways."

"Oh to be able to have one of those wonderfully foolish gut

laughs which I used to share with my friends. Now I can only see humor and feel it, but not to the extent I once allowed myself to participate in it. It was always such a release after a good laugh. Do you know those few really good laughs in your life where you could hardly stop laughing?"

"Venture further up the mountains to places you have not yet been. You'll always have a better view."

"It seems unfortunate that I have attended so many funerals lately. How sad. Not that so many of my friends and acquaintances were released from the pain and suffering of AIDS, but rather from the waste of lost opportunity for growth by the individuals, not to mention the talent that is being lost by the earth's population. We have all wondered why this must be. I hope by now I have the answer. I will assure you, it is my first question upon passing into my new life."

"Why is it so hard to stay centered on the path? Complete faith with joyous expectation!"

"The pain grows constant now and the need for writing grows stronger. My only problem is the ability to stay focused. It's hard to not let the blanket slip off long enough for concentration to occur. I dread the medicine that allows me some peace as I feel its power taking over."

"You can never turn back the hands of time. Cherish the experience as it occurs, for only memories can prevail into the future."

That last quote is on the painting I have hanging in my bedroom. Ironically, the quote has slowly faded and now has completely disappeared from the art.

Only memories prevail.

ANOTHER NEW BEGINNING

Randy loved the ballet. We had seats for opening night each season in a private box in the theater. He knew each dancer by name and admired their talents.

A few months after his death, I was at an event with friends, and a man came up to me and introduced himself. He said he just felt a need to say hello. He was one of the dancers of the Houston Ballet. After that night, we were together for two years. There was no doubt in my mind that Jim was a gift from Randy. And what a gift he was in my life. He is a beautiful soul. He was a gift that I let go and will always regret; however, I know now that it was simply not good timing.

That entire era of death from AIDS seems like another lifetime. It is now just a memory. Eighteen years after Randy's death, in 2010, I was sitting in class at Antioch University, listening to a lecture about the AIDS crisis. The teacher looked directly at me and said, "Does anyone have a personal story he might like to tell?" I was the only old man in the room, so there was no doubt he was speaking directly to me. It was an unexpected and difficult question. How was I supposed to communicate such a challenging battle in just a statement?

I asked the class to look around the room and imagine that everyone is going to die except you. "Every day of your life, I hope you will live for all of us, and do many great things to help the world." There was a long moment of silence, and I noticed that most of the class was in tears. They heard my heart. Thank you, Randy, for being there with me in that moment.

I want to be sure and give attention to the many people who still suffer from AIDS survivor syndrome. Those who experienced the pain of dealing with AIDS in the '80s and '90s often develop a new form of pain. They did not expect to live. Still to this day, they experience much greater risks of depression and suicidal thoughts than those who are negative.

If you are one of these people, please seek help. There are support groups and social groups designed to help you survive and thrive with others going through the exact same experience. A great organization to explore is LetsKickAss.hiv. *POZ* magazine is also a wonderful resource.

THE MENTAL GYM
Write Your Story; Show a Little Pride

What would your obituary say if you wrote it today? If you listened to your heart and considered a change in direction, what would your obituary say in twenty years? What would it say if you were living as you know your heart and soul wish for you to live?

A movie is going to be made about your life. Write an outline of act 1, which is your past. Then write the outline for act 2, which is what you are going through presently. And finally, act 3: your future and how the movie will end. What genre will the movie be?

Very importantly, what does the main character learn in the end? What are the lessons? What is the main lesson in this movie to inspire the world?

Everyone loves to hear a good story. Every person's story is interesting. That is quite simply the basis of every AA meeting. Write two or three funny stories about your past. Read them to someone.

According to public historian Richard Cheu, "Telling your life story is an important part of thinking about your past, present, and future." You can throw off negative feelings about your past by giving yourself a new, brighter perspective on your life. Looking back at your past is like climbing into the attic to see what is stored there; you must "find the meanings of your past."[14]

Show pride in your story. What if you hear, "Wow! I didn't know that about you"?

Draw a picture of your life to go along with the story. Only allow yourself ninety seconds to show your entire life's story. Set your phone timer. Don't think. Don't give yourself any time to plan it. Just draw.

What does it say to you?

A MINDFUL MOMENT

Find a quiet space. Sit comfortably in a chair or on the floor. Take a few deep breaths, holding them each for four seconds. Breathe into your stomach. Allow a few quiet minutes.

Close your eyes. Imagine that you see heaven far off in the distance. What does it look like? As you walk closer and closer, appreciate the glory and overwhelming beauty of it.

As the door opens, who do you see? Picture an entire community of the greatest people. Family. Friends you knew. Famous people. Great achievers.

Who steps forward to take your hand and lead you into the community?

What if they ask you, "Why are you here?" How will you answer?

Tell them your mantra. Ask them to explain it in their words.

As you repeat your mantra, open your eyes and become grounded.

---

14 Richard Cheu, *Living Well with Chronic Illness, A Practical and Spiritual Guide* (Indianapolis, IN: Dog Ear Publishing, 2013).

CHAPTER 4

Jump from the Cliff and Fall into a New You

There are many times in life when we are handed a gift, but as I have mentioned, it sometimes comes in some ugly wrapping paper. It doesn't look like a gift when it's thrown at you. It hits like an Amazon package dropping from a drone.

You have to first get up and stop the bleeding. You're allowed to scream and yell, but don't forget about the package you received. It can often take a long time to cut through the tape, pry open the box, dig through the paper, and finally find the gift, hidden deep in all that trash.

You could always choose to curse at the box and throw it away. But we all know that getting a box from Amazon is exciting. If only we could look at our struggles the same way. What is hidden in that trash?

My next personal story is not an easy one to tell. It was an incident in my life in which I was completely unwilling to find meaning or hope. The box crashed hard on my head and needed to bleed for quite a while.

A DIFFICULT STORY

In the mid 1980s, I started a small production company with two partners. We had all worked together previously and were good friends. We became even closer friends as we overcame the lessons of paperwork, legalities, marketing, staffing, and all the other necessities of starting a company. We were young and fairly naïve to business practices but ready to tackle the world with our enthusiasm. The drive to success is often blind.

One of my partners, Nancy, became such a close friend that on her wedding day, she asked me to walk her down the aisle. Her father had died several years earlier. It was a beautiful day filled with joy and, of course, high production values. That evening, Nancy and her new husband left for a week of honeymooning.

On her first day returning to work, she and I stayed a little late to catch up on a few projects. As our day was ending, I heard someone come in the front door and start talking to Nancy. She sounded anxious, and I assumed her new husband had come to surprise her. I heard her say, "Bill is in the back." Suddenly, behind me in the doorway, Nancy said with her voice shaking, "Bill." I turned and saw a man wearing a mask and holding Nancy by the neck. He had a gun to her head.

That was the beginning of a long night of robbery, trauma, and physical and sexual abuse. It was a date that will forever be glued in our memories. Following the incident, we had many weeks of trauma therapy and a search for any type of healing. Some stories are truly unexplainable in regard to their purpose. There will often be post-traumatic stress, sometimes delayed. Life moves forward, whether you choose to move with it or not.

The police eventually caught our intruder, and after two long court trials, the defendant was sentenced to two life sentences with no parole. We were told by the judge that there was no explanation for why we were still alive.

⊙ ⊙ ⊙

I had no idea at that time that 1989 would begin as the worst year and end as one of the best.

What was the dessert that was coming? I certainly did not have a desire to keep my fork. And yet one beautiful, life-changing positive came from that experience.

Just a few weeks later was the synchronistic beginning of my *Heart Strings* journey. I was in the audience of a conference, listening to a producer talk about a national AIDS benefit that was going to tour the country. I instantly felt the calling to speak to him after his presentation. Two weeks later, I was hired as associate producer, and within a few months, I was on a bus for a year.

All of this was proof once again that there will be new life after death, if we choose to find it. AIDS took away all of my close friends, and then, through *Heart Strings*, it gave me an entirely new set of friends. They were with me to listen to my goodbyes and then embrace me with a new hello.

Life is unpredictable. Keep your eyes open. Keep your hope afloat. Keep your fork.

Following that tour, the next two years were very much focused on taking care of Randy. I returned to Times 3 Productions for a while, but it proved difficult, particularly with Nancy gone. Eventually we sold all of the company to our third partner, and I began the adventure of trying to start a new company called OneTV.

OneTV was well intended but not the brightest idea in the world. It was a television show not unlike any of the morning talk shows but for the gay community. We had two professional hosts from New York City, and we told stories related to topics of interest to that audience. The downside of the idea—and remember, this was the early '90s—was that it would be on a cassette tape delivered in the mail once a month. We knew no networks at that time would air it. It was well before the Logo channel.

My partner, Coky, did our East Coast marketing, and I made all the trips to LA to try to gain support from big names in television. Once again, that was the hidden blessing in this not-so-blessed idea for a company.

Through the marketing journey of OneTV, I met people in Los Angeles, and I began to think of moving to this city of angels. I recognized that I was unhappy in Houston because it was a constant reminder of all the friends who were no longer living. At that time, I also believed that I probably had little time left on this planet. Why not move out to Hollywood and have some fun before the disease added me to the list?

In January 1995, I loaded up a truck and moved to Beverly. That was the year I turned forty, so I could wave goodbye to my difficult thirties as I literally drove away from them. It was a challenging move. I had moved many times in my life, but this time I was saying goodbye to my career, my home, my assumed future, and most of all, it was a final goodbye to all the friends I had lost and the lives we had together.

I still had that strong courage inside, taught to me by bullies when I was fourteen. Once again, I was picking up my art supplies and taking one step at a time. It will never be as difficult as that first time learning the lesson; however, my "art supplies" now required a very large truck.

We are naturally creatures of habit. We find comfort in the routine of our lives and all the actions and objects representing that comfortable routine. We usually don't like goodbyes. From a young age, we grow attached to our toys, and even when we outgrow them, we don't want to let them go. We move on from relationships, jobs, friends, and homes, but even when we know it's time to move on, the goodbye is difficult. However, there comes a time when "it's time."

Los Angeles was my new future. My thirties were "over." My life in Houston was "over." That career was "over." Whether these things offered the best or the worst moments of my life, I will always celebrate them. They made me who I am. They made me strong.

Moving away and moving on can be rewarding and challenging. I chose to move on. I chose to walk through the unknown, and I had no idea what a glorious life lay ahead. I moved in with my close friends Carl and John, who were vital in introducing me to all the advantages LA had to offer.

⊙ ⊙ ⊙

I often ask my clients, "If you had no fear, what would you do?" The irony is that life can become so much more than we ever dreamed of, but only because of overcoming the fear. Fear is just a road sign showing we are about to accomplish new goals and meet new, incredible people.

If you stop believing and trusting and you lose hope, you will never know the glory of what's to come.

Everywhere I have lived in my life, I have formed incredible friendships. Because of that, I am saddened by all the thousands of cities where I have not lived and where there are so many potential friends I will never meet. I cannot imagine if I had never left central Ohio and gotten the opportunity to know, love, and grow from so many new people. If you are ever struggling with the decision to move, simply focus on the potential friendships waiting for you.

Life is about sitting up on the cliff's edge and looking down below, contemplating how, when, and why. We wish we could swing over the chasm and check out the terrain before letting go of the rope, but we don't get to do that. Instead, we have to take the leap of faith. There is often blood-rushing excitement in taking that leap and moving forward. New adventures are exhilarating and frightening at once. Life is emotion.

Before jumping, contemplate what is below that will catch you. There is often a meadow of friends, family, and love. Old experiences might also catch you and rebound you back into the air.

Author Anne Lamott says, "You can't think your way into becoming yourself."[15] There are points in our lives where we are confronted with the decision to become our true selves.

Jump.

THE MENTAL GYM
My Fear Isn't Funny

Write something funny about your worst fear.

Write it to the music of your favorite childhood song.

Or write a new song.

Write a children's story about it.

Write a funny poem or short story.

Children embrace life without question or prejudice, but as adults, we are weighed down by our histories and the narratives that we have buried in our minds like concrete. Try a new approach. Act like a child! Go into a K-Mart or Target. Where do you head that makes you happy? What items bring wonder, delight, intrigue, or peace?

A MINDFUL MOMENT

Sit comfortably with your feet firmly on the floor and your arms wherever comfortable. Before you start the mindfulness exercise, think of one big accomplishment you would still like to conquer in your life. Perhaps it involves love, career, adventure, health, or spirituality.

Is it a secret you have not yet discovered? If so, simply imagine an aura around an "empty" but promising space filled with hope.

Once you have determined that goal, slowly close your eyes and begin the four deep breaths. In for four seconds, hold for four seconds,

---

15 Anne Lamott, "Becoming the Person You Were Meant to Be: Where to Start," Oprah.com, November 2009, https://www.oprah.com/spirit/how-to-find-out-who-you-really-are-by-anne-lamott/.

and release for four seconds. Allow the breath to go all the way to your stomach, not just your lungs.

Sit quietly and simply appreciate the quietness. Once you are calm and at peace, picture an image that reflects that element of your life you would like to achieve. Think of it far off in the distance. Create its glorious and beautiful color and glow. Take a few minutes to concentrate on it.

Next, begin to walk toward it. What is the feeling in your body as you approach it? What are you stepping through to get to it? Is it changing as you get closer?

Imagine stepping into it, and through it. What reveals itself to you? What are you seeing? Repeat your mantra from chapter 1's Mindful Moment.

Spend as much time in this beautiful space as you would like. When ready, slowly open your eyes. Sit quietly and appreciate this experience you have just had. What is one word to describe it? Say that word three times.

CHAPTER 5

Owning Choices: I Methed Up Everything

Before I finally took the leap to move from Houston to Los Angeles, I went to see a therapist in an attempt to process that major decision. What stuck with me most was his comment that when we take on the challenge of a new city, between six weeks and six months later, we will think we have made a huge mistake almost 100 percent of the time. He told me to own it. "When it comes, just say, 'Wow. Here it is.'"

He was correct, and when the moment hit me, I felt such great comfort in knowing what he had told me. His advice was applicable to almost all challenges. There will always be moments of regret, sadness, and confusion. Just pause, be mindful, and be comfortable saying, "Here it is."

He also told me to be prepared for a new type of community.

"People in Los Angeles are always busy. They can't tell you why, but they are always busy." That is 100 percent true.

He taught me to meditate in order to deal with the new stress of being around such busy people, but he taught me in the form of hypnosis. The sound of it scared the bajesus out of me. I was fairly open minded, but that sounded way over-the-top woo-woo. The ironic part is that you cannot fully experience the benefits of hypnotherapy unless you are completely willing. So I eventually figured I had absolutely nothing to lose. (He promised not to make me walk like a chicken.)

He convinced me that the best way to explore my mind was to first allow myself total relaxation. He explained that *total relaxation is effortless.* Relaxation is the absence of effort. So it is in releasing all effort that we become relaxed.

To begin our sessions, he had me close my eyes and imagine myself on a beach. The waves would slowly roll up to my feet, and then I imagined my thoughts drifting back out to the ocean with those waves. Each time the waves came in, they would take more stress and, indeed, effort with them as they slowly washed back out.

Then I would concentrate on different parts of my body. I would focus solely on my legs becoming extremely heavy. Then my arms would also become heavy weights in the sand. Then my shoulders, and eventually my head.

Once I was relaxed, he would count backwards from ten to zero. On each number, he instructed, I would feel twice as relaxed as the previous number. He counted slowly. The degree to which I felt my body become relaxed with each number was intense. Finally, at zero, he would pause and then say, "Effortless." He never used that word until I was at the point of complete release of stress. That word signified hypnosis. I never felt hypnotized. I simply felt completely relaxed.

A very strange thing happened to me while I was seeing him. I was at a party, talking to some friends, sipping a glass of wine, and two women were having a conversation behind me. In the middle of a sentence, one of the women casually said, "Effortless." My body went completely limp, and I almost dropped my glass of wine. I was programmed to relax when I heard that word. Fortunately, that response has gone away, and my head is not falling on my keyboard as I type that word today.

It has been twenty-eight years since I saw that wise teacher. To this day, if I have a problem falling asleep, I put my mind on the beach and step through the relaxation techniques. When I start to count backwards from ten, I have never reached six before I fall asleep.

Guided imagery, also referred to as creative visualization, is similar to hypnosis. The brain has incredible power over the physical body. If the brain believes it, there is nothing to stop the body from following through with the imagined instructions given to it.[16] Your brain causes panic, which causes chest pain. Your brain causes fear, which brings shaking. It can also cause calmness and relaxation.

At the same time I was seeing that therapist, I discovered a book titled *Executive in Passage* by Donald Marrs. His book gave me hope and courage to change my life and make the move. In the book, Marrs states, "We, each of us, must act as bearers of gifts into each other's lives, as if we might have made an agreement before entering this life to meet in this hour, at this place, and to offer our own particular kind of being. And in our giving we help the other find love."[17]

I decided to let him prove it. I wrote him a letter stating that I needed help in my new transition. I asked if he would meet me for lunch once I moved to Los Angeles. I heard back from him immediately with an enthusiastic yes. I will always remember the exact location and table where we sat and shared stories and cried. So many emotions emerged in that one setting. I was humbled that he was willing to take this time with me. I was proud of myself for reaching out and asking. I was also proud that I had read the book and related to his stories. I was impressed that he felt an emotional response to mine.

Donald explained that there will always be huge advantages to taking a leap in life. He pointed to his new wife, and they kissed each other. I never saw them again. That was twenty-eight years ago and remains as vivid as if it were yesterday. He lived the essence of his book.

---

16 Kathy Gruver, PhD, LMT, RM, *Conquer Your Stress with Mind/Body Techniques* (West Conshohocken, PA: Infinity Publishing, 2013).

17 Donald Marrs, *Executive in Passage, Career in Crisis: The Door to Uncommon Fulfillment* (Los Angeles, CA: Body Techniques (West Conshohocken, PA: Infinity Publishing, 2013).Barrington Sky Publishing, 1990).

STARTING OVER CAN BE HUMBLING

"Create your bridge. The bridge is a new consciousness that forms between the life we know and the life we can create. Just as difficult as integrating the parts of ourselves that we don't like, it's also very difficult for us to integrate the parts of ourselves that are deeply precious and of great value." Eva Archer-Smith

Moving to Los Angeles meant a new career search. Finding a job was a struggle. Having a resume that said I had owned a production company was not the asset I hoped it would be. I discovered that people thought I would want to take charge, so one day someone in an interview suggested I take that off and simply say that I had experience as a production assistant.

I went so low as to interview to be an office temp at entertainment companies. It was an eye-opening experience to witness firsthand how people in those positions are treated in the entertainment world. Here are two examples of real phone calls I had:

November 12, 1995

ME: Good afternoon, Disney Corporate Travel.

CALLER: Is this someone who can help me, or just the receptionist?

ME: This is "just the receptionist."

CALLER: Well, it would certainly be helpful if you would say that when you answer the phone.

ME: Good afternoon, this is just a worthless sack of doodoo who can't do a damn thing for you.

November 19, 1995

ME: Good afternoon. Disney Corporate Travel.

CALLER: Is Pat there?

ME: She is on vacation today. Would you like to talk to someone else, or would you like her voicemail?

CALLER: Well, I don't want to be put on hold for twenty minutes like you always do.

ME: Okay. Well, Pat will be back at nine in the morning, so I'll put you on hold for eighteen hours instead. And you might want to order some food. She has two other callers waiting. Please hold.

From the owner of a company to receptionist. Three months later, I took a position as a production assistant with Dick Clark Productions. I worked on several awards shows, including the American Music Awards. I could write a new book about the stories from that job.

My first day at work, I saw three large dogs walking around the office. I asked the woman next to me, "Are all these dogs Dick's?" Without looking up, she replied, "No. The one on the right is kind of friendly."

The executives in the upper ranks of that organization were extremely difficult to work with. One day on set, one of the executive producers asked for a bowl of only red M&Ms. When the PA delivered them, the producer threw them across the room and shouted, "I said to put them on the left side of my chair!" That was just one of many stories. We lived on pins and needles. It doesn't take a genius to recognize what I learned from that experience. Basic human skill number one: treat others the way you would want to be treated.

I recognize the misguided thinking behind that behavior was to "toughen up the newbies" and teach them survival skills in that competitive industry. It was very similar to my fraternity hazing. But again, there was also a horrible culture of superiority and "earned" ego—who gets to piss on whom. It all seemed completely silly to me, 100 percent because of what I learned from the bullies in high school.

At age forty, I knew this was childish. The high school bullies taught me courage, my fraternity brothers gave me strength, and now Dick was simply showing me who was a . . . Well, you get it.

The complete opposite of that behavior was taught to me five years later by Mitt Romney. He told our team at the Olympics that every single person's job is just as important as yours. So stop and say hello to the doorman and ask if he needs anything. Be kind to all of those around you.

My Dick Clark life was short. As soon as I could find another position somewhere else, I was gone. I became a production manager at the Walt Disney Company, working in special events. We put on huge productions around the country for animated film premieres. As in so many areas of my life, I met several close friends at that position, and I had amazing and rewarding experiences.

There was, however, a hidden side of my move to Los Angeles that I will get to later—once again, a secret.

BUT THEN ANOTHER DOOR OPENS

My move to Los Angeles gave me many more opportunities than I could have ever imagined. After leaving Disney, I took a position as manager of special projects of ceremonies for the Salt Lake City Olympics. One experience was deeply planted in my brain and would be there for me just when I desperately needed it a few years later.

THIS IS FOR ZACK

Opening Ceremonies for the 2002 Olympics began at 6 p.m. on Friday, February 8. It could not have started more perfectly. As if a stage manager had instructed the crew to "stand by for snowfall" as the lights went down, a light dusting of snow drifted down on the stadium. It was a thick, fluffy snow like we used to catch on our tongues when we were children. I instinctively caught one on my tongue that night.

The snow lasted the precise few minutes of the transition into the first musical number.

Every detail of this production had been planned to the microsecond. It had been almost three years since the creative was conceived, and now, thousands of man-hours later, 4.6 billion people were tuned in to watch it. None of us dreamed that Mother Nature would perfectly coordinate her own special effects and sprinkle a little powdered sugar on our heads.

Bundled in my blanket and seated among 55,000 other frozen attendees, I felt as though my heart could warm the entire state of Utah. In that moment, I vividly remembered that day on the playground when I looked up at the sky and said out loud, "This will be the hardest day of my life." In this moment in the stadium, in response to that, I looked up and said out loud, "This will be the most joyous day of my life." I will never forget that moment.

The lights went dark, the music began to swell, and like a magical sunrise, the entire stadium, along with my spirit, burst into color and pageantry.

The audience members had each been given specially prepared packets with several gadgets and gizmos to be used throughout the show. The first one to be opened was a white hooded poncho. Therefore, all 55,000 of us were dressed as a white backdrop for the production, blending into the snowcapped mountains behind us.

We also had flashlights to be used at a key moment in the show, and large folded cards that opened up to spell out messages and graphics across the stadium. It was important not to swap packets. Each one was unique to its own seat.

But what was most unique about each seat, I thought, was that 55,000 spirits had all come together at this stadium at this point in time to celebrate this glorious peacetime tradition. From all around the world, these people had gathered in this spot to join hearts and hands. It was just five months after the tragedies of September 11, making the symbol of what we did here all the more powerful for the world to see.

I had learned a lesson earlier that day that made this all even more grand and profound for me personally. There was one soul among us who was not in the seats and was not wearing a white poncho.

Let me go back one month.

I was on the road with the Olympic Torch Relay from New York City to Boston for the first three days after Christmas. I was in the car with Mark Walker, one of our media spokespeople, who traveled for the entire sixty-five days of the relay. Mark often stopped unannounced at elementary schools to surprise the classes, show the children the torch, educate them, and motivate them about the Olympics.

On our first day out, we stopped at a couple of schools, and Mark demonstrated to me that his job was so much more than informing the world media about the torch relay. It was also about enlightening the minds of children and encouraging them to dream. Any one of them might someday be an Olympian.

Later that night, in Providence, RI, we pulled up to the celebration site. It had been a long day of traveling. We were greeted by a very sweet elderly woman named Molly. Molly had an extremely thick Irish accent. She hugged us and told us how special it was to have the torch in her hometown. She explained that her grandson Zachary was signed up to volunteer, but he was sick in the hospital, so she was filling in for him. Zack had lymphoma.

Mark asked Molly if she would like to get a photograph with the torch. Instantly she began to cry. She said that it would mean the world to Zack if she could bring him a photograph like that.

She refused to let us go to the store for her to get a camera, or even drive her. "Don't move, darlins!" was her plea. (This was obviously before we all had cell phones.)

When she returned, we took several pictures and talked to eighty-three-year-old Molly for almost an hour. Before we left, I gave her an Olympic Torch Relay pin to give to Zak.

A week later, I was back in Salt Lake City and received copies of the photos with a lovely note of thanks from Molly. As I read it, I could hear her saying, "It warms my heart," which she had repeated to us many times in that beautiful accent that reminded me so much of my own Irish grandmother.

I knew then that our jobs were not necessarily to overwhelm the world. We would be entertaining 4.6 billion viewers for Opening Ceremonies, but something else had become blatantly obvious to me. Our jobs were also to impact individual dreams. We were there to encourage everyone, children and adults, to reach inside themselves for inspiration. We would do that by celebrating those who were accomplishing their dreams in the Olympics. This was not just about sports but about hope and inspiration.

I realized that I had never truly internalized our theme, "Light the Fire Within." Igniting some inner passion serves to spark a dream in others.

On this day of February 8, the day of Opening Ceremonies, I was obviously very busy. I was literally in my office for three to four minutes just to grab some notes. As I was running out, the phone rang, and I answered it in a rush. It was Molly. The timing was unbelievable. Very slowly through her accent she told me that Zachary had died that morning. He died holding the pin I had given him. His last words were, "I'm going to the Olympics."

Molly asked that I please pray for Zack's soul when the flame ignited that night on the Olympic cauldron. He would be rising to the heavens with the torch, the boldest symbol of world peace and Olympic unity. It would be his proudest way to say goodbye.

"It would warm my heart, darlin'," Molly cried.

Then she said something that changed my life forever: "Please always remember, Bill, that life is not about the millions of people who are watching the Olympics tonight. Life is about one person helping one person at a time."

I will never forget Molly or the lesson she taught me. Our greatest accomplishments, even the Olympics, are not about how many people we reach. Life is about reaching just one person.

The Opening Ceremony was viewed by the world. But one person was special. I helped Molly bring joy to a little boy I never met. That is more important than all the rest.

When the cauldron was lit that night, my heart was so swollen I could hardly breathe. Fifty-five thousand individual lives, all speeding in separate directions, were crossing at that moment in the stadium. Even more incredible, 4.6 billion people were watching us. I was united with every one of them. From down the street and across the world, we were all there to celebrate the most powerful symbol of the human spirit. In my own small way, I had helped to produce it. How fortunate I was that my life was crossing this landmark. How fortunate I was to be able to help. I knew right at that moment that I had to write about it, if for no other reason than I had to thank Zachary and Molly by propagating the lesson they taught me.

There is an infinite number of ways to reach the gold medal. I could not help but think that everyone in Rice-Eccles Stadium that day moved slightly closer to achieving a dream.

All problems seemed petty. All disagreements and frustrations melted away. Overwhelming emotions poured out of me in tears. As we each lit our small flashlights and waved them in unison, it was clear that the world is a great place—all of it symbolized by a single flame, which, like the rest of us, seemed to keep reaching and grabbing for the heavens for hope and peace. I thank the people of Salt Lake City for letting me be a part of such a beautiful and glorious event.

Never ever fail to light the fire within. The light that radiates is glorious. I learned that from the 2002 Olympic Winter Games in Salt Lake City. I learned that from Zachary.

It is difficult to stop briefly in our busy lives and remember to help someone. The smaller the act seems, perhaps the greater the investment. A phone call. A pat on the back. An anonymous compliment. A smile. That lesson from Molly and Zachary was a huge impetus for my transitioning from the world of large events to sitting in a small room as a therapist . . . so that I can help one person.

I never imagined that five years later, I would also be diagnosed with stage IV lymphoma. Through the many rounds of chemotherapy, I often prayed to Zachary. I never knew him, but his existence changed my life. Molly thought that I changed him, but the change was fiercely in the opposite direction. He was there with me, holding the Olympic pin. He had a very short life, but it had incredible purpose.

I don't tell this story to praise anything I did. I simply gave away a little pin. But it had such a profound affect, in a small way for Zachary and in an enormous way for me. We never know when we might touch someone. It might be simple, but it might change a life. Our own.

THEN I METHED UP EVERYTHING

Just days before that ceremony, Human Resources had a seminar for all of us titled "Life After the Olympics." They warned us that we might experience depression or other struggles. They explained that we were all in the world of special events, completing the largest special event in the world, so it would feel like going downhill after that job ended. All of a sudden, it would be completely over. Adding to that sadness, most of us would also be without work for a while, and we had just earned some money. Time and money is a deadly combination.

I did not pay much attention to the lecture. I had never experienced depression, so in my mind, I was in the clear. However, once I moved back home to LA, I very quickly learned that the deadly combination of time and money is multiplied by a thousand if you add drugs to the equation. The automatic solution to depression is more drugs . . . and the automatic response to more drugs is greater depression.

My favorite song while dancing was "We Found Love" by Rihanna. When the beat kicked in, it was heart pounding. I still feel it whenever I hear that song. Recently I was listening to it on the radio and realized the lyrics were about the relationship between me and the drug. "It's the way I'm feeling I just can't deny. . . . But I've gotta let it go."[18]

I spiraled down quickly, and then one night I was out having a great time partying, and a man came over to me and said I looked like I was having so much fun. I told him I had just done some drugs. He made one short statement that changed my life forever.

"Good luck with that, you big loser."

Loser.

My body froze. I was immediately right back on the playground with the bullies calling me a loser. Only this time it was the truth. I was a loser. To this day I wish I could find that stranger and thank him for saving my life.

I was reminded of the courage those bullies had taught me, and I could use that courage to no longer be a loser, a word that is still difficult to speak. It was one of three words my father refused to ever let us use: *loser*, *fool*, and *stupid*. That is probably the reason for its intensity for me personally.

I had developed a life of "fake" courage. I've always thought of alcohol as liquid courage. Many of us remember the first few times we had a little too much to drink. We felt invigorated and invincible. Some people become addicted to that instant relief, moving on to other drugs

---

18 Rihanna, Album *Talk That Talk* (New York, NY: Def Jam Recordings, 2011).

that make courage even stronger. We all know it is false courage, which sadly leads us in the opposite direction of true courage—to liquid, injected, or snorted courage.

There is an expression in twelve-step programs: "Recovery from an addiction is like having sex with a gorilla. You're not done until the gorilla is done." Even though the year of 2002 was my rock bottom, when I came to the realization that I had to get sober, I knew that I had been hiding an addictive personality for many years, once again in the form of secrets and substances. I could now finally breathe and be honest.

My gorilla was done.

When the bullies taught me courage, it was an easy courage. I wanted to run from Ohio and explore the world. At the time, it didn't seem so difficult. Now I know that courage means risk, uncertainty, and vulnerability. Addiction recovery taught me that it also means emotional exposure.

I began to step into courage like I had never done. I became willing to give up control of my life and do what others told me to do in order to stop my addiction.

So, what is true courage?

You can't buy courage at the store. You have to earn it. Each and every step of our lives brings more courage. I learned and earned it from the bullies on the playground, and I firmly believe that those of us who overcome addiction develop some of the strongest courage a human can possibly muster. Ironically, taking step one—admitting we are powerless over the fake courage—is courageous. Getting sober also takes enormous endurance. It is such a difficult struggle to not go back to the comfort of that fake courage.

"Action with anxiety is courage. Action without fear is like doing the laundry."—Harold Kooden

Anyone in recovery from addiction will tell you the importance of the new second birthday: the date marking the shift to sobriety. It is a very powerful day in which you decide to completely stop all behavior—indeed, life as you know it. You come to recognize that you are "powerless" over your life and everything, *everything*, must change. You do not know how to change, or even what needs to be changed, but you are willing to go to any lengths.

You are willing to listen to a complete stranger tell you how to begin all new behaviors. It feels weak, vulnerable, helpless, and horrible. It feels like you are surrendering your entire being. And you are. There is nothing more humbling. It begins with admitting complete defeat.

My day of surrender began with a trip to the beach. I sat there, shaking and crying. I literally did not know what to do. I looked down and saw a rock. I picked it up and squeezed it tightly. A rock. I was low enough in my life that a simple rock might give me strength. I pulled out a pen and paper and began to write:

Today is hopefully, the first day of never using drugs again.
My depression is greater than I have ever known, and I want to search my soul, make sure I still have one, and find some semblance of serenity.

Grasping for any symbol of hope or peace, I found this rock on the shoreline. I can physically hold it in my hand for strength. Even a simple rock is giving me something to grip and feel grounded.
I am squeezing it as hard as I possibly can.

I think I will look for four rocks.
Why not?
If one is giving me so much strength,
why not three more?
I could find one to each represent
Strength, Hope, Courage, and Beauty.
This first rock is clearly the rock for Strength.

Within a few yards, I found hope and courage, but I wanted the rock of beauty to stand out from all others. Several minutes later, when I finally spotted it, I reached down to pick it up, and a wave grabbed it and took it back out to sea.

My mind immediately made up scenarios to explain its escape. Was I nowhere near ready to grasp the final outcome of beauty? Was I only fooling myself that I could even think about beauty yet? Or worse, was I even being rejected by a rock now?

How dare I think I could attract anything beautiful in my life?

Or was this rock dealing with its own issues? Perhaps it was not ready to take on the responsibility of "most beautiful rock." Was it in a greater funk than I, and it chose to "go out" one more time before it had to get serious?

Whatever the reasons, this rock's outer beauty did not seem to reflect the inner beauty of the other rocks. I realized that it had no strength, courage, or hope.

I hope I see that rock in a meeting someday.

All of a sudden, I realized I was not thinking about my addiction or my depression. For just a few minutes, I was focusing on the rocks.

That day at the beach in 2003 was an amazing mirror to the day when I was fourteen and being bullied on the playground. I sat remembering what I had labeled "the worst day of my life," and acknowledged that this might be number two. I recognized the correlation between picking my art supplies off the ground and collecting the rocks on the beach. The bullies had taught me courage, compassion, shamelessness, and hope. The rocks were symbols of courage, strength, hope, and beauty. Three and a half decades later, I felt the exact same shame, emptiness, and sadness but was still blessed with the hope of courage and strength.

I now pick up four rocks every time I go to the beach. All of them are smooth and polished. They are beautiful because they have been beaten by the ocean. Just like us, they have endured and weathered the harshest of conditions and yet managed to make it to shore.

The rocks I choose are the ones that instinctively catch my eye, out of thousands of others that also survived. My choices certainly do not make the other rocks less valuable or less beautiful, but these are the rocks that call to me.

I believe that we are instinctively drawn to people. Just like the rocks, I choose people who bring me strength, courage, and hope. It does not mean that there aren't millions of others who are beautiful people, but these are the ones I have chosen. Very often, I know immediately when I meet someone who has that human connection with me. I have learned to trust my instincts.

I have learned to trust.

ENERGY. ATTRACTION. NATURAL LAW. BALANCE.

The next day, on August 28, 2003, I called my good friend John and asked him to meet me for dinner. I had something serious to discuss. He joked later that he knew just how serious it was when he walked into the restaurant and saw me with my head on the table. That is still hard for me to believe. Our friend Ron, whom I also had known in Houston, took me to my first AA meeting the very next morning.

John was not sober, but I knew he had friends that attended AA meetings, so I asked him to connect me with someone who could help. The previous day was the last day I ever put any drugs or alcohol in my body. That statement is still unthinkable (and undrinkable) to this uncomfortable and unstoppable Irishman. (Just for the record, the Irish have the second-highest culture of drinking in the world, after the Czechs. Damn the shillelagh. I thought we were first.)

Of course, when he called me right after my dinner with John, I said, "Well, I don't really need to go that quickly. Let me think about it." He ignored me and said he would pick me up at 9 a.m. So I surrendered.

As might be imagined, that meeting was not a good experience.

Everything made me extremely uncomfortable. People talked about their feelings, and they were laughing. Who laughs on a Sunday morning? They asked anyone new to the meeting to "stand and give us your name."

I felt Ron's head turn toward me and, staring straight ahead, I said, "Don't even think about it."

That demonstrates how low my level of courage had fallen. I could not even tell the group my name.

Since that day on the beach, I have been a speaker at twelve-step conventions, and I always begin by sharing that first experience. I have gone from frozen in the far back corner to standing on stage at the podium.

Just before I went on stage for one of those conventions, a wise friend and spiritual counselor named Digby asked me to express in one sentence the message I hoped to convey to the audience. I burst into tears and said, "You are not a loser."

BUBBA'S STILL DANCING

During my days touring with *Heart Strings*, I acquired the nickname "Bubba" because I lived in Texas and did not look at all like a Bubba. That nickname has stuck for many years, and still to this day, several people still call me Bubba.

When I was out partying with my friends and we would go to clubs to dance, there was always a joke. At the end of the night, when everyone was ready to leave, they would ask where I was. The standard redundant answer was "Bubba's still dancing." I loved to dance, and the drugs made it all the more enticing. They had to pry me from the dance floor.

When I got sober, I had T-shirts made for all of my friends that read, BUBBA HAS FINALLY STOPPED DANCING. But the truth was that I was just beginning to learn how to dance . . . through life.

MY EMPTY PLATE. MY FORK.
MY NAPKIN. MY DESSERT.

1. In this case, my empty plate (what was being taken away) was life as I knew it. Getting sober is one of the biggest challenges to face because we cannot imagine life without alcohol or drugs. They are not only our source of fun and connection with others, but they are our coping mechanism to drown feelings. I was losing how I lived my life, and I did not remotely understand how I could ever be happy again.

2. What was my fork? What was I holding on to that I had learned would give me hope? I was holding on to hope that others had survived this. Somehow, they managed to get through life without any drugs or alcohol. This was a complete leap of faith.

3. What was my napkin? Who and what could I count on to catch me? Every single person I met in the twelve-step programs, especially my first sponsor, Chuck. Slowly I learned to trust those wise people who kept asking to help me. I soon learned that they represented a truer form of trust than I had ever known.

4. What was the dessert that was coming? LIFE!

SON OF A BITCH; EVERYTHING'S REAL NOW

A sober life does not have anything to do with alcohol or substances. It is the removal of that and a shift toward "life on life's terms." Learning how to deal with real life in a healthy manner is what sobriety will teach us—if we are willing to learn.

Sobriety teaches us more lessons than we dreamed possible. First and foremost, the opposite of addiction is not abstinence. The opposite of addiction is community and connection. That was proven at the very first AA meeting in 1935 in Akron, Ohio. Bill W. and Dr. Bob believed that no matter how much a person tried to fight an addiction alone, it didn't work. Helping each other was the key to a strong recovery.[19]

There are many factors to their theory. Accountability to others is of course a key element, but so is our ability to take what we have learned and help others. We take our focus from isolation, lying, and pain and transform it into helping others change their lives.

Another key component is working the twelve steps with a sponsor. The steps should be inclusive of everyone and up there with the duty to pay taxes. Maybe turn "accounting" into "accountability-ing." Every detail of the steps allows for personal exploration, healing, and growth as a human being. It is miraculous to watch people grow from living the lowest life imaginable to becoming successful and proud. The biggest motivator is seeing others who have what you want: *community*.

One of the biggest reasons it is vitally important to stop trying to think your way out of addiction or alcoholism—and instead simply listen to what is told to you—is because our damaged brains are not wired correctly. The program calls it "stinking thinking." We think we can do it our way, but it is important to put our brain on pause and ask for help. Our brains have been physically damaged, and we experience PAWS: post-acute withdrawal syndrome. The symptoms often include confusion, depression, anxiety, mood swings, and many others. It makes rational thinking difficult. A long period of healing is necessary.

One of the biggest and most immediate results of PAWS is thinking we are unique. Comparing ourselves to others is almost everyone's immediate reaction: "I'm not *that* bad," "I never had *that* happen," "Obviously I must not have a problem," or "No one knows how bad it really was for me." This is true of every type of struggle we go through in life. We compare, and as they say in the program, "Compare equals despair."

---

19 *Alcoholics Anonymous Big Book* (New York, NY: AA World Services, 1939).

That dilemma was a major factor when I first got sober. Imagine walking into a room of crystal meth addicts who have been homeless and/or imprisoned and telling them that your rock bottom was someone calling you a loser.

The only thing that mattered was that I knew I needed help. I knew my soul was empty and that I was not the person I was meant to be.

SPIRITUALITY AND SYNCHRONICITY

One of the biggest hurdles for me was step two, which gives importance to a Higher Power. My past experience with religion made me extremely hesitant about this step. I questioned whether this program was a religious cult.

I now know that nothing could be further from the truth. We each determine our own Higher Power. It took me several years to fully embrace the exploration for my personal Higher Power, but now that exploration has become my greatest comfort. We will never fully understand a higher being; we simply observe how he/she/it is working—through "harmonious actions of the universe," such as the connection of the moon to the waves on the beach. Part of my exploration was contemplating whether these connections demonstrate synchronicity or natural harmony. Or is that the same thing?

I have also learned to listen to the natural harmony connecting my body and my soul. In his book *Jung, Synchronicity, and Human Destiny*, Ira Progoff explains that our bodies act by cause and effect, but our souls act through desire to work out our purpose—not to "find" our purpose but just to work toward finding it. Psyche means "soul." Psychology is the science of our souls. He says, "Synchronicities are the harmony between body and soul."[20]

---

20 Ira Progoff, Jung, *Synchronicity, And Human Destiny* (New York, NY: Dell Publishing Company, 1978).

Synchronicities are clues to our path in life. In the book, Progoff states that perhaps a more indicative word than *coincidence* would be *co-occurrence*. Synchronicity suggests that the coincidence of events in time and space amount to more than mere chance. Jung believed that the universe has been established in a way that draws the body and the soul to correspond and have a lasting affinity for each other. A phrase used by Kipling is "Just so!," and the Chinese refer to it as Tao. It is a principle that binds the entities of body and soul together.

The binding of my body and soul—is that not the ultimate goal? There is so much in the universe that we cannot comprehend. Our brains are not even close to understanding time or reason. The only answer is to find a peaceful bond between body and soul.

We know those moments of synchronicity. We feel them in our soul with great intensity and emotion. Very often we cannot explain the feeling. The awareness comes from outside of our body. Or is it inside? Or both? That is the unexplainable part of synchronicity. Perhaps we can think of each moment of synchronicity as a brilliant step toward the unfolding of our goal and our path.

While working on this book, I was having dinner with my good friends Mark and Kevin in Denver one evening. They asked me about the book. As I began to explain it, one of them interrupted me and asked what the title was going to be. Right at that moment, the waitress put three forks on the table and said, "Dessert is on the way!" I literally froze with the hairs on my neck standing tall. I knew I had the right title.

As I mentioned, I called my friend John when I needed help with my addiction. I met him in 1989 on the *Heart Strings* tour. He told me that he had always had a fascination with the number 1111. I got excited and told him that was my address, my old phone number, and my fraternity PIN number. It had come up so many times in my life.

It was much more than a coincidence. I could not explain why it kept reappearing, and John's admission brought even more importance to it. The only word I could use was *synchronicity*, but it was something that words could not explain.

There is a theory that 1111 represents the exact alignment of how life is meant to be. I trust that it is always moving me forward with an energy that I call my Higher Power. Eleven eleven continues to reappear in my life. Very often, I'll get a text from someone at 11:11, telling me they are looking at the clock and thinking of me. As soon as we're told to be aware of something, the brain is wired to constantly recognize it.

John died suddenly of a brain tumor in 2004, just months after my sobriety. Because he was a beautiful singer and performer (almost winning Star Search one year), we produced an elaborate memorial for him. Our amazing and beautiful friend Sally Struthers hosted the event, and many of John's talented friends performed. We held the memorial on 11/11.

Soon after that, I had a dream that John and my mother came to visit me. They had become best friends in heaven. I asked them to explain the meaning of 1111. My mother said, "Only you can explain it, but I want you to know that is why I named you what I did." She held up a sign that read, *W 1 1 1 1 A M*. The next day I made a sign with that image, which I have framed in my bedroom. Without the *W*, it's almost a subtle anagram for "I am 1111."

I had always wanted to get a tattoo of my mother's maiden name, Ryan. And, of course, I also wanted 1111. While creating my own designs, I realized that there is a *1111* hidden in *RYAN*. So, on the exact hour of the fiftieth anniversary of my mother's death on New Year's Eve, I got the tattoo: *1111* is lightly floating behind *RYAN*.

For a few months after, I felt sad that I had not somehow included my partner Randy, who is also a part of their social club in heaven. I was at work one day, and a woman asked if she could see my tattoo.

The *Y* is slightly hidden in the bottom of the *R*, and she didn't see it, so she said, "Who is Ran?" I said, "No, there's a *Y* in there." She said, "Oh! Randy?!"

I just about shit my pants.

That is my new word for synchronicity . . . *shit-my-pants-ity.*

SO MANY YEARS WITHOUT TEARS

Through my work as a counselor at Hazelden Betty Ford, I learned the beautiful concept of emotional sobriety. Most of us stopped feeling true emotions as we became more and more dependent on a substance. Rather than deal with all of life's emotions, we smothered them. As we get sober, we must learn what emotions are and how to deal with them.

Crying was a huge part of my early sobriety. I didn't know why I was crying. I called my good friend Jack in Houston, who had been sober for many years, and I asked him why I couldn't stop crying.

"Bill, you have always had a big pile of shit in your living room. You just put a slipcover over it and called it a sofa. Now you are taking off the slipcover and starting to dig out your shit. The stench is making your eyes water."

'Nough said.

Jack was right. As I mentioned, I had a huge hole that I had always filled with all the wrong substances, and now I was confronting who I was meant to be. That is an enormous task. I had clearly lost connection with the reality of emotions; I even had to ask someone else why I was crying.

Emotional sobriety is learning to regulate the extreme highs of emotions, such as rage, anxiety, and irritability, and the extreme lows such as depression, exhaustion, and discontent. As Andrew Susskind says, it is similar to relearning to drive a car.[21] You cannot drive with

---

21 Andrew Susskind, MSW, SEP, CGP, *From Now On* (Los Angeles, CA, 2014): www. andrewsusskind.com.

your foot pushing down only on the brake or on the accelerator. We must learn to stay in the safely regulated zone.

There is such incredible value in painful emotions. When we accept them, embrace them, and listen to them, we become more human. It is important to remember that what we are thinking is not as important as how we are feeling.

AN EXERCISE: *What am I Thinking?* *What am I Feeling?*

Stop for just a moment and focus on how you are feeling. Hold your hand over your heart. Breathe. Describe your feeling.

Emotional sobriety is the capacity to appreciate the fullness of life. Appreciate! Life is an exploration of who you are.

Concentrate on one emotion you have on a regular basis. Give that emotion a name. It is not you, so make it a separate entity. Depression is a common problem that talks to us, and we believe him. He is not real. He is a made-up character in our brain, so let's say we name him Goober. Whenever Goober talks to you, just say, "Thanks, Goober. Now shut up."

OPPOSITE THINKING

For many people, a common curse is opposite thinking. We walk into our first meeting and feel like everyone is staring at us. No one will talk to us, and then, when someone does, we want them to go away and leave us alone. We think some variation of "I'm better than all these losers, but I'm a piece of shit."

We think that way because that was exactly what our relationship was with alcohol or drugs: "I love you. I hate you."

The solution for this is the common ground between those two statements: "I trust you." I mentioned in chapter 3 that in the dictionary, faith means trust. That is exactly what the second and third step are all about. Finding something to trust and committing to trust it.

STRESS

Just as the therapist taught me before moving to Los Angeles, total relaxation is effortless. Relaxation is the release of effort. Releasing effort is the key to comfortable.

Thus, it is important to recognize stressful effort in our lives. It is possible that you have been stressed for so long that you don't even recognize the level of stress you're under. We often cover stress with more stress. And then thinking about how to release that stress is stressful.

It's helpful to first think of the areas of your life where you are most stressed. Family and friends? Finances? Work? Repairing others? Unwanted aloneness? Guilt or shame?

Don't try to release stress alone. You can't convince your brain to change by using your brain. Your brain will just stamp CRAZY and say, "Done."

Talk to others. You are a normal person going through what every normal human goes through. Most people want to help. You will recognize a healing satisfaction if you also help others who are going through a challenge. We learn so much about ourselves by the advice we give to others. Brené Brown has many incredible quotes, but one of my favorites is "Shame is given to us by others, and shame is healed by others."

Talking about our feelings is often looked down upon in our society, particularly for men. We were taught to "be strong," "buck up and be a man," and the best demand: "Stop crying, or I'll give you something to cry about." Kevin Love of the Cleveland Cavaliers began a national conversation about the taboo of emotional expression. He felt the need to talk about his struggle with anxiety. He said, "Talking about your feelings could be the most important thing you ever do, and yet it's something our society tells us not to do."[22]

> *"Highly sensitive people are too often perceived as weaklings or damaged goods. To feel intensely is not a symptom of weakness; it is the trademark of the truly alive and compassionate. It is not the empath who is broken; it is society that has become dysfunctional and emotionally disabled. There is no shame in expressing your authentic feelings. Those who are at times described as being a 'hot mess' or having 'too many issues' are the very fabric of what keeps the dream alive for a more caring, humane world. Never be ashamed to let your tears shine a light in this world."*
>
> —Anthon St. Maarten

Give yourself permission to feel rotten. Be at peace with not being at peace. Write your way through the challenge. Writing on paper slows your brain down to the speed of the pen, so you think much more clearly when you write. The best part of writing is having that journal to go back and read later in life.

Behavioral change is a pathway to emotional change. It can be healing to develop a list of pleasurable activities that alter your thinking. When working with clients, I offer a list of 200 activities; however, just researching pleasurable new activities is a pleasurable new activity to start with. There are so many simple new habits we can form that may sound cliché, but they truly help. Of course, exercise and healthy eating are important subheadings for that list.

One of the main principles of Alcoholics Anonymous and Al Anon is learning to recognize what we have control over and what we are powerless over. Recognizing "powerlessness" is the first step (literally and figuratively) to finding a glimmer of peace.

---

22 Clayton Geoffreys, *Kevin Love: The Inspiring Story of One of Basketball's Dominant Power Forwards* (Winter Park, FL, Calvintir Books, LLC, 2016)

Not long ago, I was on an airplane, and the woman sitting next to me asked which rental car company I used. Instead of saying, "Alamo," I accidentally said, "Al Anon." We both awkwardly chuckled, and then she said, "That's the company that teaches you to ride comfortably in the passenger seat and recognize that you can't drive the car." Brilliant!

Ride comfortably in the passenger seat. Life will drive the car.

It is not just a simple cliché when the readings of twelve-step programs state that if we work for it, rewards will come. Those rewards are called the promises. The basic theme of this book is to recognize that our greatest gifts come wrapped in some pretty shitty wrapping paper. Once we actively acknowledge that this might be a gift, we can begin to develop hope and unwrap our inner self.

Something sweet is coming.

Eliminating bad behaviors not only gives us the opportunity for anything we can dream up but also teaches us the courage to accomplish it.

THE MENTAL GYM

Think about an area of your life where you are most stressed. Family? Work? Finances? Aloneness? Guilt or shame? Focus on your fears, then focus on the opposite of that fear. What might allow that opposite feeling?

Write a song to your soul. One of my private clients wrote a great song titled "Mr. Hydrangea." It was a goodbye song to the flowers he had planted in his garden that died, and yet when he read it to me, we recognized that it was actually a song written to his soul . . . his own period of sadness. When he came home from his almost fatal stay in the hospital, his hydrangea had also almost died. After he clipped it, the leaves came back quickly, vibrant and green. It was a beautiful metaphor for his life.

A MINDFUL MOMENT

One of the most personally powerful educations I did at Betty Ford is directly related to my very first day of sobriety. It is an exercise I call "rock bottom." For each person in the room, I brought a rock from the beach. On the rocks I wrote their new sober birthday, and I asked them to tell the group the one powerful moment of clarity that got them to begin recovery: their rock bottom.

Start by holding and carefully examining a smooth rock. Notice the color, the angles, and the way the light plays on the surface. For just a moment, appreciate the formation of this rock.

Take four deep breaths while gripping the rock. Squeeze it while breathing in. Release it when breathing out.

Think about the history of this rock. Where did it begin? What has it been through? How is it at peace right now?

Hold the stone in your hand. Feel all the sensations of this piece of nature.

Grasp it firmly and feel all of your emotions being absorbed into the rock. Allow the rock to take them away.

Take one deep breath as you once again appreciate the beauty of this rock. Your rock.

Write your mantra on your rock.

CHAPTER 6

I'm Sorry You're Having A Bad Day. Did I Tell You I Have Cancer?

Cognitive behavioral therapy (CBT) is based on the theory that our thoughts influence our feelings. Situations, events, and people are not what make us feel a certain way. Our thoughts about the situation are.

What is the difference between a thought and a feeling? If it's a full sentence, it is a thought. For instance, "I felt like he was trying to hurt me" is a thought. A feeling is expressed in one word, such as sad, afraid, angry, happy, excited.[23]

Of course, CBT does not mean to say, "Stop worrying and be happy." One of the worst things to say to someone who is going through a trauma or struggle is "You don't have to be sad. Just think happy thoughts." The opposite is true. Let yourself be sad. Happiness can return later, but only through the process of feeling the pain first. For now, just cry. I will continue to use the expression "If we were happy all the time, we would never appreciate being happy."

We don't always have control of our thoughts, which then define our feelings. Many of them are automatic and learned from childhood. What we can control is our response to the thoughts. That is the basis of CBT. What is the counter-thought that might dispute, or embrace and process, that initial thought? In other words, think about the thought.

The entire basis of the twelve-step program is to change how we think, and step one is to stop the thought that we are to blame. Reverse

---

23 Jeff Riggenbach, PhD, LPC, *The CBT Toolbox: A Workbook for Clients and Clinicians* (Eau Claire, WI: PESI Publishing and Media, 2013).

the thought to *I am powerless over this problem. It's not my fault, and I am not a horrible person because this happened. In fact, I am incredibly strong for having the courage to change my life.*

That is the perfect example of changing our thoughts. Accept the thought as a natural, automatic response, but then recognize that it is not necessarily true and is possibly terribly wrong. Clinically, this process is called cognitive restructuring. With some time, anything learned or embedded in our thoughts can be relearned. It just takes a little time and rethinking.

Anyone going through a struggle often blames themselves. The thought is *What did I do to cause this?* In many cases, it is the same as blaming the victim of a crime. The human response, which was learned as children, is to think about what we did wrong or didn't do right. Many negative things that happen in life require acceptance, which in itself is a positive thought.

The most common negative belief is *I am a failure.* Yet we all know that no one has accomplished success without failure. Accepting failure is an enormous step of courage. Accept it and reframe the resilience. Success comes from failures. Actions might fail, but no human is ever a failure.

Nothing is a mistake. Everything serves a purpose.

There is a great chance that what you perceived as your tragedy or your weakness turned into your greatest strength. That transition does not occur simply by "looking at the bright side" but by embracing the difficulty and recognizing the results. What kept you going?

So, according to CBT, an event happens, and then how we think about it, process it, and interpret that event will determine our emotions. What we will remember are the words we use to describe the event.

In working with a woman going through chemotherapy, I witnessed her completely change her perspective in one of our last sessions. Several people had told her that chemo is poison. So she would sit through her treatments and watch the bright-red "poison" being pumped through her body. Then, one day, she recognized that this poison was saving her life. It wasn't poison at all. It was a representation of everything good in life. She began to see this red liquid as love. She imagined full doses of love being pushed through her entire body. She told me that from then on, she cried through her treatments as she accepted the love.

I often say that my year going through chemotherapy was the happiest year of my life. It was also one of the most difficult, but because I forced myself to do funny things with all the people who came to love and support me, that is the memory I hold on to. It wasn't always easy to sing, laugh, and dance, but it always ended happy. That's what I remember.

Where your mind goes, your energy flows.

MY NEXT STEP

Three months after getting sober, I was offered the most incredible job anyone could ever hope for. The position was manager of ceremonies for the 2004 Athens Olympic Torch Relay. We would fly on a private jet, taking the torch to over thirty countries. Because Athens is home of the Olympics, we would be visiting every city that had ever hosted the Summer Olympics. That included cities in Europe, Russia, China, South Africa, South America, Mexico, the United States, and so many other landmark locations. I owe a huge thank-you to Steve McCarthy and Gillian Hamburger.

I'd never dreamed that the promises could be handed to me so quickly. However, I worried about the challenge of traveling around the world and producing celebrations while trying to remain sober. I only had ninety days under my belt.

I took the position after having a conversation with my sponsor and agreeing to check in with him daily. And the journey began. It was an exhausting experience, with little sleep on the plane between countries, but well worth it for the many beautiful stories.

Because I was sober, I was able to truly allow myself to be present in those beautiful stories. I could witness and absorb lessons and impactful moments that otherwise might have been overtaken by cravings or drinking. I was able to value the overwhelming moments, have meaningful conversations, and truly learn and grow.

One of the most memorable incidents was a lesson I learned from Steve. In each city, we had a young, energetic employee whose job was to help prepare the local relay committee with all of the rules, planning, directions, and budgets. I asked Steve one day how he was able to find such friendly, kind people. It did not go unnoticed that every one of them had a genuine level of compassion and enthusiasm. He said he had a trick that he used every time he interviewed someone. He would take them to lunch and watch how they treated the waitstaff. If they were friendly to the waiter, he knew they were a good person.

Their kindness was important not only for the local committees but also for us as we arrived to the chaos of each city.

Also, for the first time in a long time, I learned to laugh again. One of my jobs was to make sure that the corporate sponsors did not display their logos anywhere for the TV cameras to see them. That is a rule of the Olympics. Never are there sponsor logos on backdrops, onstage, or anywhere else the viewing public will see them. I became friends on the tour with the advertising director for one of our sponsors, Coca-Cola. Obviously, we butted heads several times because his job was to get their logo seen as much as possible, and my job was to stop it. He was constantly trying to come up with clever ways to sneak in a little Coke, even if it was just giving cans to the announcers or runners.

While in Paris, the final torch bearer was just about to zip-line from the top of the Eifel Tower onto the ceremony stage far below. As the crowd looked up, a parachuter drifted down into the middle of the ceremony. His entire parachute had a giant Coke logo on it. I looked at my friend standing next to me, and he had a huge smile on his face. Without even looking at me, he said, "I win, monsieur."

FIGURE OUT WHAT YOU WANT

Following that amazing Olympic experience, I once again struggled with finding the next job. Just as they warned us in Salt Lake City, the end of a job this big led to a feeling of "What can possibly follow that?" Fortunately, this time, I didn't attempt to cope with chemicals.

I was offered an incredible position as a producer with a production company; however, the job was in San Francisco, and I was not in a place to move away from my support system of sober friends.

One day, I happened to be talking to my friend Eva Archer-Smith. She is not just a friend but also one of the most life-changing, life-affirming life coaches anyone could ask for. She is always filled with beautiful and healing advice.

I told Eva about my dilemma of being offered a great job but not wanting to move. She very casually said, "Take the job but don't move. Figure out what you want, and then just ask for it."

I would have never dreamed of that possibility. I drew up a creative "production schedule" as part of my pitch to the company, explaining how I could work four days a week in San Francisco and then fly home and spend the other three days in Los Angeles.

Done. They agreed to pay for the flights every week as well as a car while I was in San Francisco. I arranged a special deal with a hotel, and one month later I began two years of enjoying the benefits of both cities.

THE POWER OF THE WORD *YES*

"In a last violent protest against the hopelessness of imminent death, I sensed my spirit piercing through the enveloping gloom. I felt it transcend that hopeless, meaningless world, and from somewhere I heard a victorious 'Yes' in answer to my question of the existence of an ultimate purpose." —Viktor Frankl

Yes.

A word so simple, and yet so life changing.

While I was working at that job, I lost the most influential person in my life. My father died. I cannot say that we were emotionally close, but he taught me to be who I am. As I mentioned earlier, he was a perfect exemplar on the "stand tall, be strong and courageous" front but was not necessarily a model of the emotions that coincide with those actions. I loved him for who he was, and I knew he supported me in anything I dreamed.

Dad had been suffering from Parkinson's disease for a while, and he died exactly the way he would have wanted. He was told by nurses one day not to get out of bed. He was too weak to walk. "Stand tall and be strong" kicked in. He got out of bed, fell and broke his hip, and did not live much longer.

In chapter 1, I told the story of Dad's speech at my eighth-grade graduation, with the theme of continuing to climb life's ladder. Always find the strength to say, "*Yes*, I will take the next step."

Also ingrained in me are his reactions when my mother died. My first question to my father was "Does she still love us?"

"*Yes!*" I had never heard him say anything so emphatically, and through tears, no less.

He died thirty-eight years after that speech, but he never forgot the lesson he tried to convey to that group of eighth-graders. As he passed from this life, he was alone with my brother. He opened his eyes, looked up, said, "Yes," and died. He took the next step up.

It is not a coincidence that it was just my brother with Dad when he died. Kevin is the one who carries Dad's beautiful legacy and inspiration. His life has been devoted to giving that inspiration to others, and he is one of the most incredible, inspiring, and loving priests anyone will ever know. In his eulogy at Dad's funeral, he described his translation of the meaning of that word: *yes*. In the Bible, St. Joseph (my father's name) only speaks one word. YES. That was always Dad's motto. He kept climbing the ladder of life.

AND THEN THIS HAPPENED

Not long after Dad's death, I had one of the most shocking and defining moments of my life: a diagnosis of cancer. Stage IV Hodgkin's lymphoma. (At first I didn't realize how bad stage IV was, until I found out what stage V is.)

This statement will seem like it's completely out of a fairy tale, but cancer made me happier than I had ever been.

One day, seemingly out of nowhere, I was told that I couldn't work for a year. I couldn't go anywhere, and I might not feel so great. So I sat and I thought. And then I thought some more. And then I thought about what I might think about next. I had no choice but to face it: cancer, fear, hopes, and my entire life behind me—and hopefully ahead.

My new situation gave me nothing but time, and that time transformed me. It overthrew the idea of time and replaced it with timelessness. Cancer forced me to feel the intensity of my life. The disease that could have taken my life instead brought me a much bigger, fuller life.

I had been ill for several months before my diagnosis. My groin was so painful that I couldn't bend over to tie my shoes. My leg was swollen, and I had fevers and night sweats almost daily. My primary physician, Dr. DeFoto, was extremely supportive and sympathetic, and yet he had run out of ideas. I had a lymph node removed and biopsied, but the results came back negative. Finally, after several months, he suggested I see an oncologist for more tests. He felt that the lymph node had lied. By this point, the cancer had advanced into my bone marrow.

I got the news on Christmas Eve. The oncologist, Dr. Gould, was kind and compassionate while he told me that I had Hodgkin's lymphoma. My first thought was to say, "Merry Christmas to you too.

I'm sorry I didn't get *you* anything." But then, after a long pause, which he allowed me, I looked at him and said in all seriousness, "Life's taught me that our biggest challenges can become our biggest blessings. I'll be anxious to see what good things come from this." I meant those words. I also meant to hide behind them because suddenly there seemed to be no future. I found myself with nothing but the moment in front of me. There is nothing sharper in this world than the moment.

There was another huge reason that the diagnosis was a blessing. The uncertainty of the pain had been haunting me for months. I now had an answer.

The pain of not knowing is so much worse than the diagnosis.

Each person's life is like an enormous scratch pad where we have written notes, personal comments, and stories. We call it our memory. My new forced introspection allowed me the rare and beautiful gift of being able to sit down and read those notes. Generally, we skate over the surface of our feelings and life itself, thinking we will someday go back to process it properly. Meanwhile, deep inside us, an ocean churns, and our internal stories grow powerful. When our lives are bustling past us, who has the time to reflect on the what-ifs and the what-coulds? We barely have time to deal with the what-the-hells.

So, I began to reflect on my life, which bloomed into a ravenous hunger to share and talk and write. Writing led to art and photography. I ignored the college degree I had in design and the snobbish sophistication that came with that, and instead I created cheap and silly scrapbook art. Matter of fact, "art" is hardly an appropriate description.

It all became a journal that I called *Lymph Notes*, which eventually developed into a blog by the same name. Based on my old scratch pad, this became a new script for my current life. There was a lot of editing and updating to do from the old stories. Writing by hand rather than typing was important to me because, as I have said, when we write by hand, it slows down our brain to the speed of the pen. It opens up time for new thoughts that might not have transpired.

I enjoyed the introspection, and I also enjoyed the not-so-deep thoughts that made me laugh and made for good storytelling. And then fear struck. Was I loving this drama and this attention too much? Was I suddenly turning cancer into a selfish obsession? I called my oldest sister, someone I love and respect and who has a background in counseling the sick. Her response was "Bill, I don't think anything that makes you love having cancer can be all that bad for you."

She was right. I was letting a crazy notion interfere with my excitement and enjoyment of making *Lymph Notes* a new chapter for my future. I wrote a lot of serious and honest truths but always allowed myself to have fun. Once I began to laugh, I knew I would be fine. I had also, at this point, given those around me the permission to have a sense of humor about my cancer, and that made the laughter all the stronger. It never ceased to amaze me that we were laughing at something that strikes terror in any sane person. You're sick when you have cancer, but you're really sick when you laugh at it.

It had never occurred to me that positive thinking is simply a matter of deciding to think positively. That note never appeared anywhere on my scratch pad. We generally allow the negative what-ifs to rule. Instead, why not also give credence to the what-ifs that offer a happy ending? Take any day-to-day situation at work or home, and consider the problematic outcomes, and then consider the best that might happen. Even if the outcome is destined to be negative, think about the positives that might come from it. Everything happens for a reason. Try to discover and envision that reason.

I will say it many times without hesitation, just as I told the oncologist: my greatest gifts in life have come from my most difficult challenges. Some challenges are given to us; others we take on ourselves. Taking risks can only lead to new opportunity. Sitting comfortably through life would be boring. I like to describe the challenges as life's cliffs. Sometimes we jump, and sometimes we're shoved off. We free-fall in a space of uncertainty and have no idea where we might land. The true definition of courage is having the faith to believe in ourselves, particularly when fear is the strongest. Jump and there will be an amazing meadow somewhere down there to land in. There always is when you choose to search for the positives. Remember, too, that if that meadow turns out to be a big pile of shit, get up and get out and jump again. At least it caught you softly.

It suddenly occurred to me while examining an old journal that I had sometimes landed in a meadow in my life and never opened my eyes to see the beauty of it. That is exactly why this time of peace was so powerful. It made me look up and look around and see all incredible details I had missed.

Lymphoma was a painful boot in the rear that sent me on a long, fearful flight, but the meadow is spectacular. There are so many reasons why I needed this cliff in my life, and I know for certain that I will never recognize or understand most of them. Those unknowns are what keep us humble. Perhaps, if for no other reason, our cliffs are given to us simply to confront the unknown. Otherwise we would never advance. I believe we are all here to learn lessons, so there must be a method for us to learn them.

We're unlikely to say, "I think tonight, instead of watching my favorite TV show, I'll go upstairs and learn a lesson." We are all creatures of habit. Habit becomes comfortable. Comfortable routines get in our way.

Our minds are programmed to make assumptions based on our experiences and how we have always perceived the world. When our brain is confronted with new stimuli, it begins to reorganize and recategorize. The best way to begin to think differently, and to see the world from a different perspective, is to put ourselves into a new environment. Sometimes we don't have to. The universe does it for us.

Dale Chihuly is an incredibly detailed artist whose colorful and intricate glass sculptures have been exhibited all over the world, including the 2002 Olympics where I worked. He did not discover his sculptural genius until a car accident led to the loss of an eye and forced him to perceive depth in a different way.[24] Without that "kick off the cliff," he might never have discovered his new meadow, and the world would have never celebrated his art. He makes my scrapbooking look like, well, scrapbooking.

HAPPY CANCER

I was very surprised how much I cried through that year of cancer. It often came out of nowhere. I can honestly say, however, that I do not remember a single tear of sadness. That is written several times in my journal. The tears were a way for me to reconcile the love that was difficult for me to express to myself and to others. Crying is a definite awakening of our spirit. Many times I couldn't explain the tears. They came out of nowhere, but some very powerful feeling came out with them.

Thoughts about important things in life turned into overwhelming emotion. I'm sure that a combination of a weakened body and fatigue were strong factors in that. But once again, as my sister said, *if it made me feel that good, it couldn't have been that bad.*

I will never forget sitting on the edge of my bed one night after chemotherapy, staring at the sky. All the windows were wide open, and a full moon shined soft white light into my bedroom and onto my skinny little legs. (I was probably glowing more than the moon from the chemo.) The garden was filled with crickets. I don't remember ever hearing crickets in Los Angeles before that night. Something deep inside of me told me that everything in life was perfect. I will never be able to convey the feeling, but it was overpowering. Everyone and everything I had ever known was telling me that life was beautiful. I was peaceful and happy, and so much of it came from my thinking, writing, feeling,

24 Dale Chihuly, www.Chihuly.com, www.chihulygardenandglass.com.

crying, and laughing (and life-threatening toxic mediation).

When I look back and see how cancer made me a happier person, I remember several simple ways it did that. In my reorganization and my rewrites of the old scratch pad, I started digging through some personal documents I had written and filed away. I discovered wonderful lists like "Things I am most proud of" and "Things that I hope to accomplish someday." And my favorite: "Good things people have told me." Take a few minutes sometime to write those. You will look back on them and smile. I was in need of a little ego, and those lists helped me.

One day I found a box of photos labeled, Pictures of My Happiest Moments. I stopped and took the time to fully appreciate them. I was so grateful that I had made that box several years earlier, never realizing that someday I would have cancer and nothing better to do than sit and relive each of those happy moments. I took a selfie of myself with the photos so I could add it to the box. Truly one of the happiest moments. All thanks to the emotional intensity of chemotherapy.

I made a series of business cards, which I called my *C* cards. They were in response to all the people who kept telling me to "play the *C* card."

Each card had a large red *C* on it and one phrase. These were a few of them:

- "I'm sorry you're having a bad day. Did I tell you I have cancer?"

- "Shampoo?"

- "You're not really that boring. It's just chemo fatigue."

- And for my friends: "I'm so sorry, Officer. I'm on my way to help a friend in chemotherapy."

I went online to find other people in the world of cancer who might appreciate the cards. To my surprise, when I Googled "Cancer, Funny," there were almost five million posts. By the end of my reading,

I was laughing and crying, and I realized that I hadn't felt better in weeks. Medicine?

A report in *Science Daily* found that humor is one of the greatest assets in healing and stress reduction. It also found that employees reported higher job satisfaction when they worked for someone who used humor and that "if employees view their managers as humor-oriented, they also view them as more effective."[25] This was even more true in medical settings where pain and depression were a daily part of life.

A woman by the name of Christine Clifford founded CancerClub. com. She is also the author of *Not Now. I'm Having a No Hair Day*. She even markets products for people with cancer who love to laugh. She brought me much joy.

One of my biggest inspirations was Scott Hamilton. Most people remember him as the 1984 Olympic gold medalist in figure skating. Soon after that, he was the brain behind *Stars on Ice*. Scott's approach to his cancer was inspiringly fun: "Stay positive, keep it fun and friendly, and have the quality of life that you deserve. I learned that you can choose how you feel on a particular day, and if you just turn something slightly—like you might turn a piece of glass and get a rainbow—you change your perspective."[26]

As a young child, Scott developed a mysterious illness that caused him to stop growing, but he continued to take skating lessons and play hockey. At age seventeen, financial pressures forced him to quit competitive skating until an anonymous couple sponsored him for the 1980 Olympics.

Scott believes we have three choices: succumb, adapt, or evolve. Of

---

25 Canisius College, "Laughter is the Best Medicine," ScienceDaily.com, January 26, 2008, www.sciencedaily.com/releases/2008/01/080124200913.htm.

26 Scott Hamilton and Ken Baker, *How to be Happy (Even when you have every reason to be miserable)* (Nashville, TN: Thomas Nelson, 2008).

all of the amazing quotes throughout his book, *How to Be Happy*, this is by far my favorite: "With what I've endured, if I can be happy, anyone can. I'm a short, bald, half-neutered, chemo-d, radiated, male figure skater. What choice do I have but to be optimistic?"

I cried so many times while reading his book. He was incredibly inspiring in fueling my belief that it was okay to laugh and get through my cancer with my own constructed positive attitude.

To prove my belief in the synchronicity of a god and the power of coincidence, just a few months after reading his book, I was sitting in a Starbucks at LAX airport, waiting for a flight. Sitting at the table next to me was Scott Hamilton. I was frozen. I was crying. I was staring at him, trying to figure out some manner to explain how much he changed my life. I didn't want to say something that he had heard a million times. I wanted him to recognize my sincerity.

He kept glancing up at me.

Then he got up and ran from the table. Instead of flattering him, I totally creeped him out.

I hope he will read this and recognize two things: my sincere appreciation for him, and I was not hitting on him at LAX.

MY APPROACH TO CANCER

Every time I had a chemotherapy treatment, I would ask a different friend to take me. I made a ritual of it. (As a producer, it was only natural that I would want to work from a script that I created.) During the treatment, I asked each friend to read small pieces of *Lymph Notes*, and then we would talk about it. Following a short discussion, I would ask them to write a page in the journal about their feelings. Every single one of those pages is so powerful, as was the intensity of the friendship at the end of the day.

The writing was generally followed by a comedy movie, and at the end, we would take funny photographs with the medicine, the needles, or any medical device we could find. In the later months, I brought costumes for them to wear. It became a full production. At one treatment, as my friend Kristen was dancing in a drunken Disney princess outfit, the nurse said, "What are people going to think about our clinic when they hear this laughter?" Kristen froze for a minute and then responded, "They're going to think that some people laugh in the face of danger and enjoy life no matter what."

The joke is so close to the hope.

It almost seemed selfish when I had so much fun. I became addicted to the generosity of others once I learned to accept, appreciate, and enjoy it. To make myself feel better about it, my sister and I made gift bags for all of those chemo escorts.

One of my biggest gifts during cancer was my roommate Rob. Clearly, he had been given to me as the greatest inspiration I could have asked for. He was kind, generous, funny, and caring. One of the most powerful stories of my journey was a night in July 2008. Rob thought I needed to go to the ER. I didn't want to go. I just wanted to sleep, but Rob insisted he take me to the hospital. When we arrived, they immediately put me into intensive care because my blood pressure was incredibly low. They told me I could have possibly died that night.

While in the ER, Rob asked me if I had eaten any of the cheesecake we had in the refrigerator. We laughed so hard: I was lying in the emergency room, and he wanted to know if maybe it was the cheesecake? He said his stomach hurt and wondered if it was related. The nurse ended up checking his "tummy ache," and within a few hours Rob had an appendectomy. We both spent the night at the same hospital. Turns out we were each a huge blessing for the other.

Throughout the months, other people, in their generosity, offered me so many beautiful things to help in my recovery. I was open to anything that anyone wanted to throw at me. I tried Reiki, which is a Japanese technique to move calming and healing energy through the palms of the practitioner. I tried acupuncture and yoga. I very much enjoyed biofeedback, which was definitely the beginning of my exploration into positive thinking. The computer seemed to know when I needed it and how much. Thank you, Chad Allen. You gave me the basis for this book.

My friend Carl brought me "Alabama mud," a concoction of herbs and healing foods blended together and guaranteed to not let my hair fall out.

Definitely my favorite offering was the generous gift of breast milk, thought by some to be a cure for many ailments. (I did not take it on tap.) A very well-meaning friend pumped her breasts and brought me several bags. I would put it in my coffee in the morning. Admittedly, it almost made me throw up every time.

After I tried both of them, my oncologist asked me to stop anything that I was taking internally. Not only could they have a bad interaction with my meds, but I didn't know what was really in the mud, and he emphasized that breast milk was not created for men in their fifties. (There are so many directions to go with that humor that I won't even begin.)

Because of my daily search for new areas of excitement, and to make every attempt to not focus on any discomfort I was having, I routinely discovered new things that made me happy. What a blessing. If all else failed, I could always step out into my garden, perhaps a blatant metaphor for my meadow.

When I told Dr. Gould on that day of diagnosis that I looked forward to the gifts of having cancer, I was determined to find them. It wasn't hard. They were there all along. All I had to do was find a new platform from which to view them.

During the chemo sessions, my body became very different. Fluids built up in my stomach, and my arms and legs became very thin.

Perfectly timed, I read a quote one morning from Glenn Close: "Vanity and happiness are incompatible." It made me reflect on the photograph I had been using for my blog. It was a small, bald baby bird looking over the edge of a nest. My body image was exactly like that little bird, and yet the only thing he saw was hope for a whole new future once he could fly out of that nest. Never once did he stress over what he looked like. To him, he was perfect, and one day he would fly. From that morning on, I kept telling myself that one day soon, I too would fly again.

I had decided that the last entry in my journal would be the day I found out I was free of cancer. On that day, Friday, September 19, I transcribed a long and difficult search through my feelings. I cried harder than I had cried all year, and for the first time, these weren't tears of joy. The experience was ending. For all the reasons that I have tried to explain in this chapter, that was sad to me. I ended and closed the journal with "I don't think I ever imagined just how powerful this recording would be to my life. It is a capsule of incredible love and beauty. And now this chapter is over. Good night, sweet cancer. Good night."

Later that night, at a celebration dinner, my friends all laughed that my reaction was the height of drama, and I laughed with them; however, in some way, it showed that this very personal journey could not be understood by others. Possibly, there is no way I can ever explain it. That is the definition of a personal journey. But I want to try, in an attempt to help others who are just beginning a new journey.

More than any other lesson, that year taught me that I can endure any cliff. Fear during the free fall is human nature, and I can accept that as well. But it is always a little easier knowing that there will be no crash landing.

I left several blank pages at the end of my scratch pad, anxious to see just how the "cliffhanger" ends.

WHO ARE THESE BUS DRIVERS,
AND WHY ARE THEY AFTER ME?

A topic often discussed in cancer groups, both for the patients and the caregivers, is what to say to someone with cancer. When we have a loved one or friend who breaks the news to us, our brain immediately scrambles for the right thing to say.

First and foremost, embrace the gift they are giving you. It takes courage for them to talk about it. Elizabeth Harper Neeld says to simply say, "I'm sorry," and if appropriate, "I love you."[27] (Not "I'm sorry, and if appropriate, I love you.")

Remember that nothing you can say is going to make it better or heal them. Simply let them know you will be there for them. Thank them for their vulnerability.

Yet there are many standard lines of inappropriate things to say.

- "You'll be fine."

- "You can beat this."

- "I know someone else who had it, and they are fine now."

- "You're strong."

- And the worst of all: "You never know. You could get hit by a bus tomorrow."

A woman in one of my groups decided she was going to write a book titled *Who Are These Bus Drivers, and Why Are They After Me?* It would summarize all the well-meaning but crazy things people say when they themselves feel uncomfortable.

---

27 Elizabeth Harper Neeld, PhD, *Tough Transitions: Navigating Your Way Through Difficult Times* (New York NY: The Abbey of Gethsemani, New Directions Publishing Corp, Time Warner Book Group, 2005)

MY EMPTY PLATE. MY FORK.
MY NAPKIN. MY DESSERT.

1. *What was my empty plate?* What was taken away from me? The greatest course that was taken away was my career, and thus my identity. I no longer had the energy (or desire) to endure the world of entertainment. Once again, I was thrust into the uncertainty of unemployment, which I always say is worse than cancer. Like many others, I had always felt that what I did was who I was. My career and my identity were tied together. There I sat, staring at my empty plate.

2. *What was my fork?* What was I holding on to that I had learned would give me hope? Once again, all the lessons I learned from the bullies, all the lessons I learned from sobriety, and all the lessons I learned from moving to new cities and new areas of my life were still in my spirit. There was never a question of having hope and faith that I would survive and thrive.

3. *What was my napkin?* Who and what could I count on to catch me? It took this major illness for me to recognize just how large my napkin truly was. I had a vast group of family and friends who were more dedicated to me than I ever knew.

   My napkin was also the knowledge that being thrust into uncertainty had always been the greatest impetus for me to rediscover myself. My present brain, however, was shouting, *Really? Again?*

4. What was the dessert that was coming? An entirely new life that I would have never dreamed of.

◉ ◉ ◉

Here are two stories that display hope during cancer.

I once facilitated a group for mothers and sons who were facing cancer. Some of the mothers had cancer and their sons were there to support them, and some of them were sons with cancer, and their mothers were there for support.

One of the members was an eighteen-year-old boy who had a brain tumor. I asked him how he perceived his future. What he told me was so profound that I will never forget it. He said that he looked at his life as if he were floating in the ocean. Any direction he looked, he had an endless, vast sea ahead of him. He could swim any direction and discover new territory and new adventures. "But for the present moment, I just need to learn how to swim."

The next day, another young man in the group took him to the beach and photographed him floating out in the ocean. At the next meeting, they came laughing and remembering how much fun it was.

Another story is one I was fortunate to hear from the parents of a young boy who had leukemia. The doctor told them that they should try to explain to their six-year-old that he was going to die. After studying the perceptions of death for a child his age, they devised a plan to try to explain it to him. The parents went into his hospital room and pulled the curtain around his bed. They stood on the other side of the curtain from him.

"Can you hear us?" they asked him.

"Yes," the young boy answered.

"We want you to know that you will always be able to hear us. And we will always be able to hear you. We may not always be able to see each other, but we can always hear each other."

Obviously, this was probably more healing for the parents than for the young boy. It was important that they felt the comfort in knowing they would always hear his voice through what has to be the most difficult struggle possible: losing a child. That is the one challenge in life for which I don't believe there is a silver lining. Many parents will create nonprofits or foundations in honor of their child, which often helps many others, but there is still no way to balance the loss of that child.

PAIN VS. SUFFERING

Pain is a part of life. As I have said throughout the book, we decide how we choose to perceive it. No matter what, it makes us stronger, and if we allow it, it will direct us down a new path. We just have to be willing to search for the purpose.

I had a young client at Cancer Support Community who told me that in his opinion, pain is our stepping stone to our higher power. He said, "That which is painful is the most important thing in my life."

I have talked about Viktor Frankl. Throughout his horrific experiences in four concentration camps from 1942 to 1945, including Auschwitz, he searched for lessons of spiritual survival. His parents, brother, and pregnant wife all perished.

Frankl, a psychiatrist, brought meaning to his horrific experience. He argued that we cannot avoid pain, but we can absolutely choose how to perceive it. We can search for meaning in it and move forward with a renewed purpose. Throughout his experience, he remained firm in his belief that his perpetrators could take everything from him except his mind. They could not control his thinking.[28]

"It is this spiritual freedom—which cannot be taken away—that makes life meaningful and purposeful."—Viktor Frankl

Pain is often physical, but it can also be emotional, as with heartache, depression, anxiety, or grief. Suffering becomes the negative stories that fill our heads as a result of the pain. All of the maybes, what-ifs, and shoulds. *Did I cause this? Could I have prevented this? What will happen*

---

28 Viktor E. Frankl, *Man's Search For Meaning* (Boston, MA: Beacon Press, 1959).

now? Why, why, why? Part of our human brain immediately shifts to this thinking. It is natural and human. I call it disasturbating.

As children, we embrace life without question or prejudice; we are enveloped in a golden light of curiosity. But as adults, we are weighed down by our histories and our past narratives. Our egos want to have their way. They insist on perfection, which turns into suffering. No one is perfect.

Suffering occurs when we stop listening to our souls and spirit and stay focused on our egos.

We are each the source of our own suffering. We often reach for the future or for the past rather than trusting the harmonious actions of the universe right now. We crave fear over what might happen, and we get overwhelmed with all those could-have-beens from the past.

My grandmother believed that suffering serves a significant purpose: to help the souls in purgatory get to heaven—suffering for the salvation of others. She believed that to be her purpose. It was her way to be of service, and that belief, that service, and her religion brought her comfort. Strangely enough, it validated her pains. Did that invalidate her suffering?

The last time I spoke with her before she died, she sat with me on the sofa, rubbing my hand. She had just gotten out of the hospital and had a colostomy bag by her side.

She told me that if I remembered her saying anything, it should be this: "People keep telling you to eat this or don't eat that so that you will live longer. I'm sitting here, ninety-five years old with my piss in my purse, and I can tell you one thing: eat whatever you want and pray that it takes you early. All of those other people have not 'lived longer' like they're telling you to do. I have, and it's not pretty."

She was living at the time with her youngest daughter, Aunt Monnie, who was listening from the kitchen. Aunt Monnie responded angrily, "Mother, you keep saying you wish you were dead. When is it you would have liked to have died? At eighty? At ninety? When?"

Grandma shouted, "Thursday!" She then whispered to me, "You should have tasted her lasagna."

I had always been told not to take candy to Grandma because she didn't eat sweets. So I immediately asked her how she could give me this advice about eating whatever I want even though she never ate candy. Her response was priceless. "Oh, honey. I eat candy all the time. I just always told people that because they only gave me the cheap stuff."

I miss you, Grandma.

THE MENTAL GYM

Exercises to Reflect on Who You Are Right Now

What is it like to simply sit still for five minutes? You don't have to meditate, just sit still.

Once quiet, what are questions you might calmly ask? Don't stress at all about the past, and don't get into the solutions. Simply indulge in existential wonderings:

- Who am I when I . . . ?

- Why am I . . . ?

- What am I . . . ?

- When am I most . . . ?

- Maybe I'll ask a fellow employee to lunch. (Make it someone you rarely talk to.)

- If there were one object that truly symbolizes me, what would it be? Where might I find it? (Choose a store in which to find that object.)

- Maybe I'll compliment someone on the elevator. (Watch how it makes them feel. Watch how it makes you feel.)

- Maybe I'll take a different route to work.

- Maybe I'll ask people what creative ideas they use in their jobs. (Keep a list of the best ones.)

A MINDFUL MOMENT

Set your alarm one night, or stay up very late and go out into your yard. Try lying on a mat, or you can sit comfortably in a chair, as long as you are able to see the sky.

Take four deep breaths, all the way to your stomach. Four seconds in through your nose, hold for four seconds, and four seconds of release through your lips.

Be calm and appreciate the silence.

Focus on the beauty of the sky. Begin to explore the vast size of the universe. If indeed there are as many stars in the sky as there are grains of sand on our planet, the universe becomes too large to comprehend. What if each star has several planets with life?

Choose one star, give it a name, and ask it how far away it is from you now. What question does it want to ask you? How can you bond with this star?

Take your attention back to the entire universe. Imagine that your life is like one of these stars. You have an infinite amount of space, in every direction, into which you can soar. Where will you go? Where do you want your life to lead you? What do you hope to discover on your journey? What are your opportunities ahead?

How are you a shining star? How are you similar to the star you chose? How does that relate to the name you gave it?

Close your eyes. *Peace. Opportunities.* Breathe.

Now go back to bed!

CHAPTER 7

Those Horrible Two Words: "Now What?"

When you listen to your soul, a message will shine from the shadow of trauma. That light can lead you to transformation.

There is a beautiful wall of butterflies in the yoga studio at Cancer Support Community Los Angeles. They are all from the National Butterfly Preserve and are sold to raise money for the preservation of other butterflies. After its death, each butterfly is preserved in a small glass box.

There is a reason they are displayed there. A caterpillar goes into the cocoon thinking it could be the end of its life, just like a person with cancer, and yet they emerge so much more beautiful on the other side.

The average lifespan of a butterfly in Southern California is only two weeks. If you had just two weeks to live, what would you do with that time? Once the butterflies come out of the cocoon, they don't struggle with what to do with their lives, or finding meaning, or feeling shame or guilt. The only thing the butterfly knows how to do is stop and smell the flowers. They have no concept of suffering. (Though I've never had a butterfly as a therapy client, so I can't exactly speak to that firsthand.) They simply appreciate each moment.

It is both a blessing and curse that we humans are driven to find meaning in our struggles. Our time in the cocoon is different for each person. We struggle to find the beautiful person that will emerge. We yearn to find our colorful purpose.

Just like the butterfly, our purpose is just to *be*. To let our colors shine. However, that is never easy to discover or fulfill.

A giant crisis in our society is PTSD with military veterans. The suicide rate of soldiers is extremely high. It proves once again the importance of two huge questions: "Why?" and "Now what?"

Those questions are sometimes more of a struggle than the trauma itself.

NOW WHAT?

We sometimes hang on to our ill-fitted routines or harmful thinking so hard that we become comfortable in our discomfort. Our suffering has become so imbedded in our identity that we don't recognize the severity of it. That explains why someone may not leave a toxic position at work, or an abusive partner. Not leaving protects us from the fear of the unknown. And thus putting up with the predictable destructive behavior becomes satisfyingly comfortable. It shields us from "Now what?"

From the outside, it seems ridiculous when someone doesn't want to get out of the skillet because it might be hotter "out there"—or, an even more questionable mentality, they know it will be cooler out of the skillet but have become very comfortable in the heat. When you're in the skillet and that is all you know, you sweat, endure it, and call it home.

When I was going through chemotherapy, I became comfortable in my painful routine. I knew that I would feel healthy for one day after the treatments; then I would crash and be in bed exhausted for two days, then sick for one day, or even in the hospital. The routine became predictably comfortable.

After several months of that routine, I was sad to leave the forced excuse to be lazy. I did not want to return to the world of uncertainty. The pain was worth it. Cancer was easier than "Now what?" I will repeat that sentence because it is vital for this book: *Cancer was easier than "Now what?"*

I was perfectly happy to be in the skillet. I just snuggled up against the sizzling bacon and convinced myself that life was fine. Fortunately for my future, the fire was extinguished, and I was forced out of the frying pan.

I had been unemployed for several months leading up to cancer. Unemployment is the worst job imaginable. The stress of not knowing what I would, should, and could be doing was much more painful to my psyche than any physical discomfort to my body. Physical pain was secondary to the comfort of knowing I didn't have to do anything except what the doctors told me to do.

For me and my cancer story, the worst was yet to come. I had no preparation for the depression that was to follow my cancer "good news." I was told that I was cured. The cancer had been completely removed. Now I could "get on" with my life. What? What life? I thought my life was over. Everything is different now. What is my future?

Everyone else heard, "Cured" and was ecstatic for about a day, and then went happily back to their lives, leaving Bill to be happy as well. He wasn't. Post-traumatic stress oddly followed a part of my life that I had not yet determined was traumatic. I had enjoyed it so much that it never felt like trauma. It was far more traumatic to be told, "You're fine. Get back to life."

A "normal" person will often say to a cancer survivor, "I'm so happy you can now get back to normal." Again, though well intentioned, they do not understand that there is no "normal." The new normal is completely unknown to those who are basically being slapped on the ass again and sent out to start a new life.

> *"Everything changes with cancer—everything. Life will never be the same again. Even in the smallest of levels, something will be forever different. There is no going back to who you once were, so embrace it and grow from it and with it. Find the new you in the new space and make it wonderful."* —Lynda Wolters

I had told the oncologist on the day of my diagnosis that I was excited to eventually learn the blessings of having cancer, but now that I was within the space of learning that gift, I was terrified. I couldn't figure out the steps to take to get there.

Sadly, the entire world got a glimpse of what it is like to discover a new normal when COVID-19 was thrust upon us. One blessing was that everyone understood. Everyone was experiencing anxiety and uncertainty. With cancer, or any other personal trauma, the rest of the world still seems to be out there dancing.

One in every twenty adults in the United States will be diagnosed with cancer and survive. Survival is a good thing. That is the most important message. We survived. However, life after treatment can be one of the lowest times of our lives. All of the love we received during cancer, all the attention of our friends and family—and even our medical team, who have become a part of our family—have been suddenly eliminated. It's not unlike the military where all your buddies, all the men and women who worked together to save each other's lives, are gone. Medical teams should include a "survivor specialist," as Cindy Finch from the *LA Times* reported.[29] Oncology departments should not simply say, "Congratulations, you're healed. Now go home and be happy."

Eventually I discovered the post-traumatic growth, but it took a serious and debilitating period of time to arrive there. I learned that there are actually three phases if you choose. You can survive. You can grow. And you can thrive.

I will forever be empathic for the veterans who struggle with PTSD. It is real. It is a period of living in fear of what is to come—or what is not to come. It requires a lot of contemplation and discovery.

29 Cindy Finch, *A Problem with How We Treat Cancer–And How to Fix It*, (Los Angeles, CA: LA Times, Opinion LA, January 30, 2015).

It creates questions you never knew existed. It is a process that no one should attempt to explore on his/her own. It often destroys the ability to work, which causes new financial fears. PTSD is total and complete uncertainty.

Trauma resides in many of our struggles through life, whether it's a major illness, an addiction, the loss of a loved one, or any other serious crisis. We often don't recognize that we are in a period of PTSD. We tend to underestimate the severity of our situation. It's real, and it's a process to work through.

Step one is to feel the feelings and allow the pain. One of the greatest pains to process is grief. It is important to recognize our losses. There is the loss of normal daily innocence, the loss of the life we had before, often the loss of friends who stepped away due to fear, the loss of our previous identity, and, sometimes, the loss of our confidence. Most importantly, as I've mentioned, we must learn to grieve the loss of our assumed future.[30] Our path has moved in a new direction.

This is where *hope* steps in.

When our brains are in the mode of the four Fs—fear, fight, flight, or fuck it—we need hope more than at any other time; yet this is exactly when we can't find it.

But hope is there. It will always be there.

Remember that there will be a light. Keep your fork. Please. You can discover something sweet if you feel, process, grow, and thrive. The growth does not come from the trauma itself. It comes from the searching and discovery of a new self. Just like the butterfly.

Your love, your strength, and your hope are in your soul. They are there. They were given to you at birth. Don't ever lose confidence in them. Don't let your mind, or another person, steal them from you. Sometimes our own brain convinces itself that we no longer have hope or love.

---

30 Elizabeth Harper Neeld, PhD, *Tough Transitions*.

Hope and love are always there.

Barack Obama ran for president with the campaign promise "Hope." Twelve years later, while his vice president, Joe Biden, was running against Donald Trump, President Obama said, "Hope is not blind optimism. Hope is not ignoring problems. Hope is believing, in the face of difficulty, that we can get a better world. Hope is looking squarely at our challenges and our shortcomings and saying, despite them, through effort and will and community, we can make things better."

Exactly two weeks later, Joe Biden became the forty-sixth president.

THERE ARE NO ANSWERS UNTIL YOU BEGIN THE SEARCH FOR QUESTIONS

I was told about a lecture being held at UCLA titled "Life After Cancer" being presented by a team of oncologists. I was so excited to finally hear that I wasn't alone and there was hope.

Sadly, it was primarily about side effects and medical difficulties that could arise. It was the opposite of what I had hoped for. I learned that my neuropathy was probably never going to go away, and a host of other problems could hit me later. So much for excitement.

I thought I might still get their opinions about the emotional challenges after cancer. I felt certain they must have experienced that issue with many patients. When it came time for questions and answers, I stepped through my terror and got up in front of hundreds of people, walked over the microphone, and asked the panel how to step through the intensity of uncertainty.

One of the doctors, in a kind and caring manner, said, "Maybe you should just get a job."

There was a moment of silence, and then I couldn't believe what I said next.

"I think that is similar to telling Jackie Kennedy to just clean the blood out of her dress and get back in the parade."

There was a very long period of awkward silence. No one knew how to respond, including the audience. It is absolutely on the books as one of my most embarrassing moments. However, I was proud that I told my truth.

ETHAN

I am continually impressed by the new generation in my family. They are focused, driven, involved, and "movin' on up." One of my cousin's sons moved out to California to attend Pepperdine University for a while. At that time, Ethan was a driven nineteen-year-old who had already paid for his entire college career through his entrepreneurial skills on the internet. I had dinner with him one night, and as we finished dessert, he asked what advice I would give someone like him who is just starting life on his own.

That is not a question you want to mess up. There I sat, frozen. *This*, I thought, *better be good. After all, this kid could give me advice.*

"I don't need to give you advice," I told him. "You have already done what I would tell you. Overcoming fear and taking risks is the best advice I could give anyone. Only good can come from it."

Since Ethan had already left Ohio to venture out to California, there was no doubt that he was not afraid of risk. I wasn't sure if he recognized his own courage. Somewhere he learned that allowing that courage to bloom would set the stage for a life of open opportunity and facing those opportunities with gusto. He will be prepared for life's challenges, knowing that he can adapt and move forward through fear.

Ethan texted me the next day and said that he was "overwhelmed at the excitement of his future." How many people can make that statement? How many people are overwhelmed by the excitement of their future instead of being overwhelmed by the fear of their future? I was envious that he had such a future.

I texted Ethan back saying that I was jealous.

Then Ethan hit me with the most amazing lesson: "If you want to have excitement about your future, it doesn't matter if you're nineteen or fifty-three."

That simple text changed my whole perspective again. I recognized that I did not have the same possibilities I had at nineteen, but I had new ones, and because of my experience, I had much bigger and better ones. He should have been sitting up on stage at that UCLA conference. He had the answer to my question.

Thank you, Ethan. You asked me the question, and you gave me the answer.

Age can feel like the end, or age can feel like the beginning.

Think of it as a time to make mistakes. It can liberate you from your old ways of acting, and it can offer you a new, authentic way of living.

Surrender. Surrender to the fear and sadness. Allow it, acknowledge it, and embrace it. Surrender is a frightening word for some people because it might be interpreted as passivity, weakness, or timidity. Surrender means wisely accommodating ourselves to what is beyond our control. Getting old, getting sick, losing what is dear to us—all of those are demands to which we must surrender.[31]

NEXT

I began to think about this opportunity to explore my future. How could I use it to bring together others who also struggled with uncertainty? I called my good friend Stacia, who is a Broadway performer in New York. The world of entertainment is the crowning empire of uncertainty and "What's next?" I knew she would understand.

---

31 Amy Bloom, "What If You're Afraid of Change," Oprah.com, November 2009, https://www.oprah.com/spirit/what-to-do-if-youre-scared-of-change; Reggie B, "How to Open Yourself to Your Life's Purpose," Oprah.com.

We talked about the idea for several months, creating a mission and business plan for a new company. The idea was to develop seminars around the country to help anyone searching for the next station in life. So we called the company NEXT. We discovered that there are millions of people, particularly baby boomers, who desire to find more meaning and purpose in their lives. Retirement is often the impetus for research and discovery.

In America, we have begun a new pattern of continuing life. Baby boomers are living longer and desiring more existential rewards. They are more focused on meaning and purpose, and thus they influence the generations to come with a greater emphasis on personal fulfillment. They recreate themselves later in life. Sometimes it is the second or third recreation. There is no map for this new journey. No such infrastructure exists, and thank God, because learning and discovery is the true path of change and reward.

What makes this new journey even harder is that it stands contrary to common belief and is so different from the journeys made by generations before. Our society has always had typical traditions and rituals—and greeting cards—that tell us what is normal. Normal is birth, graduation, marriage, parenting, career, retirement, death. In that order. However, while we have to leave birth and death in the same place on the map, everything else can change order or drop out completely depending on the person. What if graduation came after retirement?

Stacia and I knew that the search is much more rewarding if you are around others who are also exploring. Listening to advice and others' experiences is motivating. Our plan was to create a stage performance involving life coaches, motivational speakers, and interactive workshops, all combined into a full-day experience.

My favorite line from that business plan was "Through self-discovery, we can learn to reach into our true selves and pull out the notepad of our lives upon which to write our NEXT story. Everything we *are* can lead us to where we should *be*. If we trust it."

We met some of the most incredible advisors along our journey. Eva Archer-Smith, who I have mentioned before as someone who assisted me personally, was extremely valuable in helping us create a script to allow people to explore within themselves. Eva's advice is life changing. We learned that everyone's journey is unique, and yet the explorations all involve very similar questions.

We hosted our first trial conference in Central Texas with the assistance of Kathy Johnston.

During that conference, a wonderful woman in the audience named Lyn Foley shared the story of her book, which she was working on at the time. A few years earlier, she and her husband had spent years planning a trip around the world. Just a few weeks before they were scheduled to leave, her husband was diagnosed with Parkinson's. They asked the doctor about taking the trip, and he advised that they cancel their plans so her husband could begin treatment. He told them the trip might be dangerous for his health.

Standing just behind the doctor was an intern, who moved her lips to silently say, "Go anyway."

They went home and talked about it and decided to take the intern's advice. They took a ten-year trip around the world, including thirty-nine countries. Together, they agreed the trip was the best experience of their life.

Her book is about enjoying life in the process of our struggles, and of course it is titled Go Anyway.32

NEXT became a full-time job for Stacia and me. I will forever be grateful to her for the work and love she put into it. Through all of those advisors, we worked diligently at creating the right questions to foster personal exploration. We even researched "What is the value of a question?"

---

32 Lyn Foley, *Go Anyway: Sailing Around the World with Parkinson's* (Round Top, TX: Round Top Books, 2012, www.LynFoley.com).

There are certain questions that our brains love, such as "What was the happiest day of your life?" "What is your favorite flavor of ice cream?" "Have you seen that Facebook video of the kitten dancing to Madonna?"

Then there are questions to which our brain responds by wanting to shut down. "What do you want to accomplish in your life?" "Why don't you just leave him and get a new life?" "Why can't you stop drinking?" "Have you seen my new Mercedes?"

Our brains like to play. Our brains love questions. That is why most board games involve questions and why people love crossword puzzles. Look at the number of game shows on television where we sit and watch people laugh and cry at questions. Rarely do we see a game show with the question "Why don't you just get over your depression?" (We leave that for *Dr. Phil* and *Judge Judy*. Again, popular shows.)

> *"When you change the questions, you change the results."*
> —Eva Archer-Smith

Begin to define your new questions. Stop asking the same old questions of yourself. From our long journey developing NEXT, here is a list of possible new questions for you.

Start by asking small questions:

- What can I do tomorrow that might make me happy or improve my life?

- What is one small step that would bring me a feeling of accomplishment?

- What do my friends love about me?

- If I got out of bed one hour early tomorrow, what might I do that could make a difference?

- What did I love as a kid?

- What if I called one person right now just to tell them I love them? What would they say? ("Have you been drinking?")

Then ask important questions:

- What does hope mean to me?

- What might bring a new purpose to my life?

- What would make me feel more balanced in my life?

- What would give me energy or motivation?

It's interesting that some of our most difficult questions are the ones for our family and friends. Choose a family member and/or a friend to ask these questions:

- "What do you think is the most important talent I have to share with the world?"

- "Who is someone that you think could be a mentor for me?"

- "What do you think holds me back?"

- "What kind of a career do you think would truly excite and motivate me?"

- "Where would you say I have made mistakes in my life?"

- "Why do you love me?"

What about your dreams?

- What is my greatest dream?

- What is keeping me from living the life that I dream?

- How would my life be different if I lived that dream?

- What is one very small step I might take toward a dream?

- Who might I ask the above questions? Who do I trust to be honest?

Be sure and take your dreams a step further than simple statements. For instance, retiring to the beaches of Florida is not really a dream. That is simply a location. What would make you happy on the beach in Florida? New friends? A new social life? Volunteering? What would be the ultimate reward? You can't just say, "To be happy" without a plan of what that means.

The ultimate goal of these questions is to help you let go of who you are today to allow the space and beauty for who you could be tomorrow.

Imagine a backpack that is constantly clinging to you. Every day, you throw worries, stress, resentments, anxiety, and fear into that backpack. It was already full from a childhood of problems. It builds and builds until it becomes way more than you can carry. Just like we do with our closets, we must learn to declutter our minds at certain points in our life. We must refocus attention and remove old thoughts to allow space for new ones. Imagine that concept: allowing new possibilities in your brain.

With a backpack full of all the reasons why you can't do *x*, you will always have excuses not to move forward. It is important to silence those thoughts. Give them to Goodwill. Put them on eBay. Upload and unload the stress of old thinking and behaviors.

Letting go of long-held hard feelings is very difficult. Letting go of our perceptions of ourselves is even more challenging, but we must reverse the negative thoughts and beliefs and instill a new confidence in who we have become. The desire to change our self-belief is step one, and by reading this book, you have taken that step.

Change is imperative for growth, both in our minds and in our souls. It refocuses how we see the world and how the world sees us. We continually let go of some elements and discover new parts of ourselves. Letting go is difficult. The alternative, however, is to not grow; to plateau; to watch life pass us by.

FUN

Having fun is both a release of tension and a release of worry. It can immediately change how we think. What is your definition of fun? Did you have ways of having fun in the past that you have not done for a long time? Would you still enjoy them? Do you have new ways to have fun?

HAVE-TOS AND GET-TOS

Make two lists of your daily activities. One list is the "Have-Tos," and the other list is the "Get-Tos." For instance, on your "Have-To" list, you might have the following:

- Brush teeth
- Get out of bed
- Drink water
- Walk the dog
- Do laundry
- Drive to work

And maybe on the "Get-To" list, you might have these activities:

- Drink a glass of wine
- Watch your favorite TV show
- Play with the kids

- Go to a movie
- Drink coffee
- Have sex

It's curious that some things on a person's "Have-To" list will be on another person's "Get-To" list, and vice versa. Consider going to work, eating, exercise, and, of course, sex.

These lists can give revelatory expression to your passions and your non-passions. Perhaps they can be stepping stones to assist you in letting go and moving forward. How can you release some of the "Have-Tos" that aren't really necessary? How can you then add to the "Get-Tos"? That is very important. What more can you add to your daily routine that is enjoyable?

Everyone's priorities, dreams, and desires for change are unique. I have a friend who worked diligently at his career for twenty-five years so he could retire at age fifty and sit on a boat and fish. It was a twenty-five-year risk to make life happier in the future, hoping for that day, but he did it. He had no interruptions in those twenty-five years at his office, and now he leads a peaceful, happy life, sitting on that boat, quietly waiting for a fish to bite.

Judgmental folks might say that he is not doing much good for the world, but that's his choice. Happiness is happiness, and he did everything to deserve this happiness in his own life.

The Dalai Lama said, "The purpose of our life is happiness."

Here are few other stories:

JOSH:

The reverse of that is the story of another friend who always wanted to be an actor and never allowed himself that privilege. His wife died of breast cancer when they were both only fifty. She left him a journal saying, "Do it, honey. Now is the time. Make me proud." He is working full-time now as an actor.

JIM:

I mentioned earlier about how I met my partner Jim. He was a ballet dancer. He was (and still is) absolutely the hardest worker I have ever known. One day, he asked the artistic director of the ballet why he was never promoted to a principal dancer. The director told him it was because he just naturally had "a renaissance ass."

Jim came home crying that day, saying he would use that butt to motivate himself. Jim went back to get his masters, was hired by the ballet, eventually became the executive director of the entire Houston Ballet, and continues to remind the artistic director whose ass is in charge now.

Talk about getting your butt in gear.

SHERRY:

After her son came to her in tears to tell her he was gay, Sherry felt compelled to help other parents who might struggle with those words. She did not accept her son's honesty with open arms at first. Now she loves him more than anything in the world and dedicates her time in honor of his struggle.

Sherry donated time and money to PFLAG (Parents and Friends of Lesbians and Gays) but always felt that she had a special creative talent that could help on a much grander scale. For many years, she was the director of sales for a skincare company and never had the courage to quit such a lucrative situation to devote herself to realizing that dream.

Then one day, out of the blue, she got downsized. After a few weeks of tears and shock, she decided to turn a downturn into a positive and take this time off to write a book for parents of gay children. She and her son together are interviewing both parents and children and compiling their stories into a legacy that she says will be her most proud accomplishment—second only to her son.

MARK:

Mark got a degree in architecture but loved singing. He sang on cruise ships for many years and grew tired of it. He worked hard to build up his own private architecture firm, but then, sitting in his office all day, he really missed performing. So he joined a local theater group and now does both. *And* he designs their sets.

JACK:

My good friend Jack was a senior VP for a large national corporation. Even though he had never been a professional chef, he decided to spend a lot of time researching what makes a successful restaurant. He and his partner, Jerry, eventually opened their own restaurant, and within two years, it became one of the five top-rated restaurants in the state of Texas. They sold it at its prime (it was a twenty-four-hour job), and Jack decided once again to change his priorities, this time to helping others. He eventually became a director of a large healthcare foundation.

◉ ◉ ◉

The common denominator between the above stories is a burning desire for change, and then taking steps.

This is the story of my change:

MY PERSONAL CRY FOR HELP

There was a single day when the despair in my soul reached a bottom. May 8, 2010. "Now what?" screamed loudly in my head. I was working hard to try to help others discover purpose, but I did not feel like I had found mine. I had an empty hole in my heart. I didn't feel that I was finding my "cancer purpose."

Just as I had done on the day of my sober bottom, I drove to the beach. This time was different. I wanted to end the pain, though I would never commit suicide because of what it would do to my family—the family who fought so hard with me during my treatments. I can honestly say that without that loving bond, there might have been a different outcome.

I went to the beach hoping that I might find inspirational rocks like I had before. However, this "rock bottom" was too severe. I left the beach and drove to a hospital. I sat in my car for hours. I wasn't sure what to do. I knew I needed help, but I was afraid. A nurse walked past my car at one point, and I opened the door to ask her to help me, but I froze. I sat in my car, staring at my phone, knowing that there was so many people I could call, but I felt like no one would understand. I also had an unconscious awareness that I wanted to suffer. It's unexplainable, but in the moment, I did not want the pain to go away. I wanted it to get as severe as possible to force a new beginning. I almost desired a psychiatric hospitalization. That way, everyone would understand how traumatic this was for me.

Finally, around 9:30 p.m., I called my oldest sister, Cece. She had always felt like my new mother, and she's worked her entire career helping others who are struggling in life. She lives in Pittsburgh, so I knew she would be asleep and wouldn't answer. That way, I could unleash a long, rambling, tearful message.

Knowing that I had exposed my pain to someone, and also knowing that she would call me as soon as she woke up, I had the courage to drive home. I had to pull over and sit in a few parking lots on the way home, but I made it. Once home, I just sat and waited for her call. At 5 a.m., I got it.

We both cried. She understood. I was right that she was the perfect person to call. She told me that there was a purpose for my pain. That was the hidden, unconscious part. I had to experience it so I could help others. She urged me to take action, find hope, and make a plan. We talked about possibilities. That very day, I called Antioch University and began my journey to be a therapist.

I am incredibly happy that I took one step toward fear and called her. Had I listened to my own head, without asking for help, the ending could have been very different.

I will continue to mention that when a tragedy happens in our lives, what we often grieve most is the loss of our assumed future. We lose a loved one or a job, or our health takes us on a new path. We are no longer going to have the future we planned. We become a ship without a rudder. When our structure falls apart, we find ourselves in a void: where we were going has ceased to exist. Of course we feel lost, without purpose.

The parade is over.

"It takes courage to grow up and become who you really are."
—e.e. cummings

Eventually, when we are in a place to make a change, we have to establish new patterns. Make new habits. Think new thoughts. Often we feel we have lost our identity. Perhaps we are just discovering it. We may wonder if anything is ever going to be worthwhile again.

Almost every author who has written about this subject mentions that we must leave something desirable behind in order to move forward. We feel stranded before we discover our path. Remember that line. We feel stranded. Then we find our path. Frequently, we cannot find the new path until we are lost. So, cherish the moments in question. Embrace the fear.

"There is only one thing I dread: not to be worthy of my sufferings."
—Fyodor Dostoevsky

Eve Ensler, the author of *The Vagina Monologues*, once told me that while she was going through severe chemotherapy, she decided in one of her early treatments that she would imagine the chemo drugs burning away all the traumas of her past. She chose to make "this poison" a medication to eradicate her horrible upbringing. She said that she soon started to look forward to her chemo treatments because they brought her amazing peace. Not only did the experience of cancer change her entire world, but the medications that most people dread gave her a new meaning in life, and a new outlook about her future.

EXCUSES AND ROADBLOCKS

In chapter 2, I discussed the healthy and unhealthy types of fear. Healthy fear will motivate us to make change, and unhealthy fear keeps us stuck—in life, in our heads, in our jobs, and on and on. We lose sight of the amazing opportunities that await us.

The world is filled with opportunities. They are abundant. The only thing stopping us from discovering them is our attitude and our fear. There are always legitimate excuses to not move forward. Money. Family. Insurance. It might also be loneliness. Is it a feeling of being inadequate? Greed? Fear of loss?

Using the metaphor of this book to describe a fear of loss, let's look at the empty plate in the restaurant that is about to be taken away. For some people, focusing on the impending dessert is impossible while they stress over the fact that the delicious meal is over and gone. What if the fear of losing the meal is so great that they can't even eat it when it is served? All joy is lost in fear of "What about when it's gone?" When you tell them about dessert, they say, "Yeah, well, that's going to be gone very soon as well." So you tell them that another great meal is coming in a few hours. "And then it will be gone," they lament.

Positive attitude vs. negative attitude. There will always be reasons to be stuck and sad, and simultaneously, there will always be new opportunities ahead to thrive.

Our fear feeds on those excuses and uses them as, well, excuses: "I'm not afraid to change. I legitimately cannot because . . ."

Most statements of fear are legitimate. The true question to ask in the beginning is "What if there were no fear and no excuses? What would I love to do right now to change my life?"

Many excuses are embedded deep inside us—false statements we have been telling ourselves for years. We must learn to release and find peace. Those past voices and experiences will live with us forever, but it is important to learn to say with all sincerity, "That is now over. That is no longer me." Most of it was never you. It was negative thoughts you told yourself, or it was others' opinions of you, or others' negative influence on you. Just as in resentments, we must learn to release the harm done to us and that we have done to ourselves. Whether it was unintentional or intentional, it no longer serves a purpose. It is in the past.

Sit for a while and ask yourself what those negative thoughts are. Write them down and dispute them.

Other excuses might be labeled as "a problem I have always had." According to Tibetan Buddhism, a problem is only a problem if we label it a problem.[33] If we look at a problem differently, we can see it as an opportunity to grow or to practice, and regard it as something positive. Is it still a problem? Or are all problems negative? Even the dictionary defines problem as something "needing to be dealt with and overcome."

We have the opportunity to once again recognize the synchronicity of opposites. *A problem is an opportunity.* It is almost always a nudge to turn our path in a different, more healing direction.

According to Dr. Robert Maurer, our brains are divided into three basic parts. At the bottom is the brain stem, which is about five hundred million years old. It performs all the basic functions like waking us up and reminding our hearts to beat. Sitting on top of our brain is the midbrain, or the mammalian brain. It's only about three hundred

---

33 Pende Hawter, Buddhist monk, founder of Karuna; *Healing: A Tibetan Buddhist Perspective*, www.buddhanet.net/tib_heal.htm, 1995.

million years old and houses our emotions. It governs our fight-or-flight responses in the face of danger. The third part of our brain is the cortex, which developed approximately one hundred million years ago. It is what makes us human.[34]

This three-brain arrangement doesn't always work together. Dr. Maurer explains that the human brain is still in the process of being formed, and thus we have confusion, addiction, memory loss, and contradictory behaviors. We tell ourselves we want to lose weight, and then we go and eat ice cream. In this context, we tell ourselves to move on and release our pain and fear, and yet it is not that simple. It stays stuck. Why?

Another reason for being stuck could be deeply embedded in this complicated brain. We learned so much in our childhood that has become subconscious. We saw and heard all the reasons our parents were stuck. It may not have been consciously heard, and it probably has not ever been processed. We witnessed their fears and emotions and absorbed them. As children, we also mistakenly accepted blame for those struggles. We saw them as normal adult emotions and stuffed it all in our toy chest.

All of that must be identified and processed. It doesn't need to be done in a painful manner. I believe that everything in our lives can be approached in a fun way. Sit with your siblings and discuss funny stories that reflect your parents' troubled minds. If that sounds sick and twisted, good. What's wrong with sick and twisted?

Dr. Maurer posits that because of the natural fight-or-flight responses in our brains, when we tell ourselves that we want to take a departure from our usual process, we trigger some degree of fear. The thinking part of our brain shuts down and becomes restricted. It says, "Just go eat ice cream."

---

34 Robert Maurer, PhD, *One Small Step Can Change Your Life: The Kaizen Way* (New York, NY: Workman Publishing Co., 2004).

That is why small, easily achievable goals become helpful. Small steps. We tiptoe around the fight-or-flight response so it doesn't wake up and cannot set off alarms. Soon, our resistance to change is weakened, and we begin to enjoy the change and its effects. In his book, Maurer stresses not only small steps but also small questions, small thoughts, small rewards, and small actions. They all can lead to big results.

The brain has many levels. Take the elevator to the "depression" floor. Or take it to the "anger" floor. The ground floor, or the basement, is always the "fear" floor. Fear is the underlying basis of most negative feelings. Why are you angry? Why are you depressed? Why are you sad? Answer them with "What am I afraid of?" Perhaps it's finances, loss of love, unwanted aloneness, or rejection. Recognizing and answering those fears is the first small step.

This is another example of a common fear: "I hate my job. My boss is so mean. But I can't leave because of my health insurance, and where else would I go?" Both of those excuses are valid, but the reality is you *can* leave. It is a huge leap forward, so begin with the very small steps of addressing the fear.

Growth cannot be possible without discomfort, but be gentle. If indeed you truly want change and are willing to attack the fear, begin with the small steps. What must you let go of first in order to take any more steps? Pride? Stability? Safety? Security? Confidence?

GIVING IN. GIVING UP. GIVING A SHIT.

Pessimism, like shame, is based around formed—not necessarily true—beliefs. More often than not, pessimism results from imposed thoughts from others, or from a darker space in our brain. It might be based on previous personal experiences that are not particularly relevant to the situation at hand.

Shame and pessimism go hand in hand. To recognize that, all we need to do is go back into our subconscious and hear our parents, teachers, or well-intentioned friends tell us,

- "You always _____ [fill in the blank]."

- "You never _____ [fill in the blank]."

- "You should think about _____ [fill in the blank]."

We hear those messages loud and clear. They are stuck in our heads, just waiting for a small ounce of shame, sadness, or pessimism to scream it right back at us. And we believe it.

The example I often use is the life of a performer. To the outside world, actors, dancers, and musicians have a glamorous life. They are onstage or onscreen, performing nightly and making people feel rich emotions. Sometimes they become famous, make millions of dollars, and seem to glow in the light of the media. But the reality is that they live a life of constant rejection. They learn from an early age that almost all of their auditions will end with "Thank you. Next." They will spend many hours and many hard-earned dollars to get headshots and agents to get them to those auditions, often several in one week, only to be cast aside rather than cast. How would most of us feel going on several job interviews in one week, knowing we had about a five-minute chance to stand out among dozens of others?

Suppose they are selected to be in a Broadway show. Their dream has been realized—until the first entertainment critic throws a harsh review at them. They lose if they lose, and sometimes they lose if they win. We all know how extremely hard the press can be on celebrities. It's as if we no longer consider them human beings. If you're rich and famous, you must be able to take criticism.

Sometimes, God gives them a huge ego to fight the fight; however, most of the time, they are human just like everyone else. Oddly enough, most performers are introverts. They feel the same pain as anyone, or worse because of their creative sensitivity. Just like most people, they have a childhood narrative of rejection in their heads, and yet they find the stamina to continue—most often because they never lose their optimism and hope.

What if they do lose it? At what exact moment does a performer decide to stop moving on? There is the old expression "Don't give up just before the miracle happens." When do they finally decide the miracle is not worth waiting for? Are they just about to hit that huge TV show, or are they "spinning their wheels"? How can they possibly circumvent pessimism? How are they able to hold on to their forks? When do they let go? I wish there were a simple answer.

A close friend of mine makes a good living as an actor. He told me that every day, he gets up and says to himself, *I am right where I am going.*

Overcoming pessimism is not for sissies. Ask any performer how they continue to move forward. How do they get over yesterday's audition so they can get up and go today? How, when, and why are they happy or unhappy?

A little bit of optimism gives us a boost to take action and move forward. You come to believe that your actions will have positive results, which transcends into more hope and motivation. A 2022 clinical study by researchers at Harvard T. H. Chan School of Public Health showed that people who are optimistic about their future will live four-plus years longer, and they have a 10 percent higher chance of living beyond age ninety.[35]

Depression and feeling unwanted aloneness are often necessary impetus for us to be reborn into a new awareness and light. The medical industry is learning that depression in aging adults might be part of a

---

35 Harvard T. H. Chan School of Public Health, "Optimism Lengthens Life," The Harvard Gazette, June 8, 2022, https://news.harvard.edu/gazette/story/2022/06/optimism-lengthens-life-study-finds/.

natural process of coming into a new light. Amid the natural progression of life, we question why we are here. *What have I accomplished? Who am I?* Slowing down and focusing inward might be the answer, albeit a painful answer at times. It can be the possible motivator for our souls to grow—if we allow it. What if you were to look at this period of reflection as the beginning of the best part of your life? What if you came to believe that the best is yet to come?

What if you stopped focusing on the what-ifs and instead appreciated what is?

DEFENSES

We all have defenses, which act as "da fences." They keep people out. We learned defense mechanisms as children to survive, creating tactics to protect ourselves in whatever circumstances we grew up in. What are your defenses? How do you unknowingly push others away? How can you begin to take down "da fences"?

Perhaps you became shy. Or the opposite: you became a bully to enhance your appearance of power. In what ways did you feel inferior to other children, or not smart enough, not athletic enough, not creative enough, not cute enough?

As we get older, we learn that no one is perfect; yet we maintain self-doubt about our inadequacies in some areas. Hopefully, we allow our talents and strengths to define us and lead us on a path that fits our comfort. However, there are always parents who decide what *they* want for their children. If you were not allowed to become the musician, the artist, the teacher, or the technical geek, then maybe your future can still embrace a new direction.

If healthcare, sales, law, or corporate management is your passion, then pursue your dreams and enjoy life. Just please remember that it is never too late.

Ask others about your defenses. Good friends know. Be prepared for answers that might surprise or disappoint you. But also be prepared to be proud.

What you're hiding is probably one of your biggest strengths.

Our defenses can sometimes lead to isolation. The consequence of pushing others away is loneliness. Loneliness is a common complaint of people who are aging, but it is also a common complaint of teenagers. It knows no age. No one wants to feel alone, isolated, without friends.

Of course, being alone is healthy at times. We all need to occasionally plug in our USB cable and take time to reboot, but sometimes it cripples the drive to move forward.

Being alone—whether it is unwanted aloneness, a desire to isolate, or just feeling alone—can be a profound detriment to your mental health. Loneliness can spark that dark depression. Loneliness is not measured by the number of people around us but by one's perception of isolation. It is a human instinct to want to be part of a group and connect to other people. When we feel alone, the instinct inside of us shouts for the company of others, like our appetite when our bodies need food.

Loneliness can be intentional, or it can happen slowly over time as you distance yourself from those you love. In today's world of electronic communication, Zoom, and cell phones, we have an immediate connection to the world, and yet cell phones are the most isolating element ever created in our society. It is ironic that we can contact anyone on our phones and instantly find information from around the world, and yet we are completely unaware of what is happening to the person right next to us.

THE MENTAL GYM
Where Do You Feel Stuck?

You have probably been reading this book because you feel stuck in life and are hoping that "something sweet is coming." Sometimes sweetness is delivered, and sometimes you make your own. Perhaps you are stuck because of a recent occurrence. Maybe it's just "that time of your life." Possibly it's boredom with your career.

Whatever the reason, you have the choice to move on. It doesn't have to happen in one giant leap. Moving on can mean taking very small steps of contemplation. Begin by asking yourself a few simple questions:

- Where were your parents stuck?

- What were their challenges and how did they react to them?

- How did they take it out on their children?

- Where are you stuck?

- How is it similar to where your parents were stuck?

- If you died tomorrow, would you be proud of how you have spent your life?

- What people, situations, or circumstances deplete your energy?

- How do you change that?

- What are the three main things you would have to let go of first in order to make change?
- What things can't you live without?

- What are the heroic feats you have accomplished?

- What do you hear when you get very quiet?

A MINDFUL MOMENT

Sit in a chair and begin with the breath work. Breathe in, hold, and slowly breathe out, each step for four seconds.

Once you are at peace, concentrate on something that brought you joy as a child. Don't think about it for very long—whatever pops into your head first.

Why is that the first thing you thought of? Why was it joyous? Who was with you?

Feel it. Laugh. Hold your heart and remember it to the detail.

The core of that joy is still inside you. It hasn't left. How might you translate that joy into your life today?

Breathe and focus on joy.

CHAPTER 8

I'm Worried that I Worry Too Much

Research conducted by the National Institute of Mental Health has shown that anxiety disorders are the number one mental health problem among American women and number two for men, second only to drug and alcohol abuse.[36] Once again, those two afflictions, addiction and anxiety, often have a direct connection. (I call it "the other AA.") It is estimated that a quarter of the entire population, both children and adults, suffers from anxiety disorders. When you throw in an international virus that completely quarantines the world, anxiety will naturally explode everywhere, as will drinking to cope with the isolation and loneliness.

There are many symptoms for an anxiety diagnosis. Some of them include excessive and persistent worry or feeling constantly on edge, often about circumstances we have no logical reason to worry about. Physical symptoms can include motor tensions such as palpitations, shortness of breath, trouble swallowing, nausea, or diarrhea. Anxiety might also display with concentration difficulties, trouble falling or staying asleep, and a general state of irritability.

Even before COVID, the epidemic of anxiety has skyrocketed in recent years, much of it due to news, financial stress, the environment, political stress, mass shootings, and terrorism. Specialists say it is due to the uncertainty that arises out of those situations. Although uncertainty

---

36 National Institute of Mental Health, "Anxiety Disorders," https://www.nimh.nih.gov/health/statistics/any-anxiety-disorder.

has always and will always be an inevitable fear, it is more intense now than ever before.

Because of social media, we are much more aware of everything happening around the world, and we find out immediately in a constant bombardment of negativity. Many people do not feel stable or secure in their future. How could we not be stressed? We are in a world of constant physiological hyperarousal.

When you add a personal struggle or trauma to that general-population anxiety, of course it makes it much worse. In some ways, that struggle might take us away from the stressors of the news, but only because we are dealing with a difficult personal challenge. It can become an even more intense anxiety.

Then again, there are some disasters that are so big, such as the coronavirus, that it brings a complete and total halt to all other stressors. Suddenly we are isolated in fear, and many of our common worries seem trivial. Do we then stress more, or do we stress less?

There are many books dedicated to releasing anxiety—books for mindfulness and meditation, identifying and being aware of the feelings, expressing the anxiety, exposure therapy, and many other types of therapy. There are books on nutrition, medications, and exercise techniques.

Step one is to recognize that you feel stressed and anxious. This state might be so much a part of your daily life that you are not even aware of the level of anxiety in your body.

All of us can benefit from finding stress-reducing methods that work for each of us. Relaxation and self-care are the most important gifts we can give ourselves and, eventually, those around us. The ultimate goal is to discover a relaxed, balanced, and healthy approach to our life today.

One of the most overlooked and yet highly effective methods of relaxation is laughter. I will explain much more about that, but first I'd like to mention the most ineffective method.

A FAKE CURE

As a counselor at Betty Ford Center, I witnessed more and more people entering the program due to an attempt to escape. They might be escaping anxiety, emotions, or fear. The escape might be through alcohol, or very often it begins with pain medication. It is commonly said that pain meds don't take the pain away; they take you away from the pain. People on these medications learn that they are also being "taken away" from all the stress and anxiety in their lives.

Prescription drug dependency has thus become a national crisis. The Centers for Disease Control and Prevention (CDC) has said that drug overdose is now the leading cause of death in the United States.[37] Worse yet, more people die from prescription drug overdose than from all the recreational and party drugs combined. That includes cocaine, crystal meth, and heroin.

People are searching for that escape. Most people who become addicted to alcohol are not seeking excitement or exhilaration. It might have started that way, but eventually alcoholism leads to lonely and isolated escape. Numb becomes better than feeling feelings. Escape from anxiety turns into escape from the world.

There is a theory that we choose our drug of choice based on what we are searching for. Usually for cocaine it is power. Crystal meth often makes a person feel accepted and confident. (It also will get your house very clean in a short amount of time.) In all of these cases, we are again escaping—escaping the fear of not fitting in, feeling disconnected, or not being strong enough. All of the traits mentioned in the previous chapter are also fuel for addiction: shame, depression, childhood trauma, rejection, pessimism, and lack of hope. Who wouldn't want to escape?

37 Centers for Disease Control and Prevention, "Well-Being Concepts," https://www.cdc.gov/hrqol/wellbeing.html.

Matthew is a young man who said that he grew up as the youngest of six boys in a military family. From a very early age, he remembers feeling like an alien on this planet. He would pray at night for a spaceship to land in his bedroom and take him back to where he was supposed to be. He hoped the aliens would land and tell him he was a failed experiment on Earth.

"Once I started drinking," he said, "I felt like the spaceship had finally landed."

CREATING CONNECTION

Human beings are created to be a part of a community. Along with food, sex, and love, we crave connection. As we become more disconnected, we build anxiety around reconnecting. It becomes much easier to isolate. To take the first step back into society, to remove the anxiety, social fear, or fake comfort of substances or alcohol and rejoin the world, is extremely difficult.

I'll repeat this here: *the opposite of addiction is community.*

That is exactly why we have treatment facilities. We allow people who are desperate or alone to begin to step back into a community and not only learn social reconnection but also explore and learn why and how they have gotten to this point.

Without a doubt, the most rewarding part of the work is watching people change. They will often come in completely broken. Perhaps they have had a tragic accident. Maybe their family has staged an intervention. Or possibly they have finally reached their worst "bottom." They are sad, quiet, and angry.

They begin to take an active part in the exercises and discussions, and soon they become eager to return each day and spend time with the group. And then, on the day of their last session, the group members each take a turn to tell the person how much he or she has meant to the group and of the opportunities that lie ahead for them. There are often lots of tears. Not only is a new life beginning, but it is also a much more enriched life than they have ever known. It's a new beginning like never before.

They then learn to build a new community through meetings. It's a shame that the entire world can't learn the lessons discovered by those who step through this difficult struggle and become reconnected. I am so lucky that I learned those lessons and was given the opportunity to learn a new kind of community and to now offer what I learned to others.

I learned so much more from our group participants than they could ever have learned from me. These are just a few of many group members' quotes I have jotted down:

- "My brain is a neighborhood. When it's dark, I shouldn't walk alone in that neighborhood."

- "When you take 'me' out of 'blame,' you only have blah blah blah."

- "Humility is not thinking less of yourself, but thinking of yourself less."

- "This program gives you the paint and paintbrush. When you leave, you have to learn to paint."

- (A woman in the group was an avid surfer. I asked her what she has learned from surfing that she might compare to sobriety.) "Always keep your eyes on the horizon."

- "I've come to realize that when I'm taking my walks, if I look down, I count my steps, but if I look up, I count my blessings."

- "I always realize too late that I'm doing just fine."

- (When asked, "What do you want your tombstone to say?") "Stop looking down at me. Look up."

- Artist: "Rather than the frantic drug-addict art, I now do one brush stroke a day. The painting is titled *One Day at a Time*. It will never be completely finished."

- "I've decided my life is like a Picasso painting; it's much nicer when I step back and look at it."

- "A saint always has a past, and a sinner always has a future."

- "So often, we spend money we don't have on things we don't need to impress people we don't like."

- "I'm so OCD it drives me crazy that the three letters are not in alphabetical order."

JUST TODAY

Addiction is just one example of a tragedy that can turn into an enormous blessing. A tragedy will often bring a halt to some of our old anxiety. We suddenly learn that all that shit doesn't matter. We discover what *does* matter.

The flip side is that we have a new direction to take our anxiety. There are new things to worry about that we never even thought about. For instance, in the case of addiction, "I will never again for the rest of my life be able to have a beer?!" That is the basis of the main philosophy behind the twelve-step program: "One day at a time." A perfect example of out-of-control anxiety is the phrase "for the rest of my life."

"One day at a time" works for every type of fear and anxiety. All I should focus on is today. Just today, I can stay sober. Just today, I can survive my bereavement. Just today, I can work through the pain, the uncertainty, and the doctors' visits.

> *"I have known a great many troubles, but most of them never happened."*—Mark Twain

There are a few other roadblocks that might make progress difficult.

JEALOUSY

Comparing ourselves to others is a human instinct. One of our most basic ways of feeling good, or feeling bad, about ourselves is by comparison.

In some ways, comparison is healthy. It can motivate us to work on areas of our lives that might be lacking. However, it is not healthy when we are already in a depressed mood and the comparison makes us feel even less connected or lower self-esteem.

Nothing on the planet has ever charged a bigger sense of comparison or jealousy than our current addiction to social media. It is filled with "teaser clips," which are basically distorted little pieces of (maybe) reality from others' lives. Not only does it show us the most amazing feats and accomplishments, but it is known that tech companies prioritize those beautiful accomplishments in our news display. This algorithm feeds on that human instinct to compare and multiplies it by a thousand.

It used to be that teens compared themselves to others at school. Now they have the entire world to compare themselves to, all day long. They get addicted to it. We all do.

There are healthy, beautiful, and comforting parts of social media. We rediscover old friends, make new friends, and find joy and gratitude in some people's accomplishments. Congratulate them. It is vital to discover who you are and how you are able to help others.

When you go through a difficult challenge like addiction or the loss of a career, you don't normally post that with extreme pride and enthusiasm on social media. Yet how many people might you help? How many others might be able to help you? How can that challenge become something that others are jealous of? What do you eventually post about it, if at all? Are there small rewards that make you proud?

What about when you pass someone on the street who seems perfect? Good for him or her. You will never be that person. Look at the next three people you pass. You will never be them either, but you probably don't want to be. All of this is unhealthy comparison.

I have always believed that when we are jealous of others and desire what they have, we must remember their entire "package." Would you really want to trade places with that entire person, or do you just want his/her car, looks, or job? Admittedly, sometimes the answer might be yes, but we can only judge from the other side of the fence, peeking over at the pool. We never really see what trouble lies inside.

Would you ever look at someone's misfortune and envy it? Of course not; however, we often admire and respect the character that sometimes develops from it. Many people have discovered and accomplished a new set of dreams because life took them in a new direction and they embraced it. We neglect to see their difficult journey, but we become jealous of the results. That can be healthy. It might motivate us into an accomplishment that we are indeed capable of. Again, healthy comparison can inspire us toward growth.

It always makes me smile when someone says, "You're so lucky." "You're so lucky because you get to travel since you don't have a family." Or "You're so lucky that you get to have a family." "You're so lucky" goes both ways. You're lucky if you do, and you're lucky if you don't. The key is to recognize the lucky parts of your life and embrace them rather than focusing on the unlucky parts.

The perfect example of that is my story earlier about cancer survivors ending up ten times happier than lottery winners. When was the last time you heard someone say, "You're so lucky because you had cancer." Nothing could be closer to the truth when it is discovered.

Loretta Breuing says in her book *Habits of a Happy Brain* that if we truly want to feel good about ourselves, and we want to compare, we should compare ourselves to our ancestors.[38] Perhaps you wish you had a new car and you see a friend on Facebook who just bought a

---

38 Loretta Graziano Breuing, PhD, *Habits of a Happy Brain* (Avon, MA: Adams Media, 2016).

beautiful Jaguar. That's great. What if you had to go across the country in a covered wagon? Once again, life can always be better, and life can always be worse. True happiness comes from comparing yourself to you.

PRIDE

What are you proud of? Don't ever lose that pride. You deserve it. We have all accomplished great things in our lives that we have every right to embrace.

And then there is ego, which loves to walk us across the healthy line of pride. Don't go too far. Watch out what you post, too. How much of your ego is telling you to click "post/send"?

Most people think that the word *anonymous* in AA means that we don't say last names, or talk about anyone outside of meetings. That is true, and we avoid ever disclosing someone else's sobriety. However, the true meaning of the word, according to the Twelfth Tradition, is humility. No one in the room is better or worse than anyone else. An old-timer with thirty years is no more important in the room than someone with one day. We are each humbly anonymous within the room. There is no judgment, no comparison, and no jealousy (ideally).

RESENTMENTS

The dictionary defines resentment as "bitter indignation at having been treated unfairly." Yikes. Harsh words, *bitter* and *indignation*. We could also add *fester* and *malignant*. We hold on to the pain, and it spreads inside of us.

When we hold resentment toward others, it triggers a very strong emotion, which is often deep inside and denied. Eventually, the harm done is never to the person we resent; we are attacking our own self-image. The underlying fear inside the resentment is having a conversation with our lower self, and it unconsciously keeps us from moving forward. Even worse, it grows the longer it is denied.

Overcoming resentments takes a few uncomfortable steps, but once again, nothing of value comes to us without a few steps of discomfort. Feeling the outward anger is a sign to dig deeper. Why are you feeling so angry? Why are you keeping this inside? Why are you blocking the road to being happy?

First of all, recognize the feeling, own it, and state it or write it: "I am feeling [sad, hurt, angry, anxious, afraid]."

Going back to the twelve steps in recovery, the fourth step includes resentments, and within that self-reflection is a column labeled WHAT'S MY PART IN IT? That does not necessarily mean "What did I do to cause this?" It could possibly mean "Why am I feeling this way about this incident?" or "Why can't I release it?"

Many people who have undertaken the steps are familiar with the quote "Holding a resentment is like drinking poison and expecting the other person to die."

One step to releasing the emotions might be to speak to the person. Expressing our feelings is a huge release. What if you approached the person with an amends, as in the ninth step? "I apologize that I have been holding a resentment for you. I discovered that I was actually feeling hurt because *x*." Keep the focus on your feelings rather than what this person did to you. Vulnerability is uncomfortable but so valuable.

Transform the resentment into a learning experience for both you and the other person.

Many resentments are valid. For instance, if you were abused as a child, how could you not hold a resentment? The goal is to acknowledge that it happened, process the pain, and recognize that the past cannot be changed. Part of the process is to somehow allow forgiveness in your own mind. As difficult as it sounds, try to understand the pain the abuser might have been experiencing.

In no way am I justifying such horrible behavior. Eventually the goal is to release and forgive. Most importantly, forgive yourself. Allow yourself a new freedom. Returning to a quote from Viktor Frankl in the opening of this book, "When we are no longer able to change a situation, we are challenged to change ourselves."

LONELINESS

COVID changed our society in so many ways. It is a global phenomenon, and yet it has also been a very personal experience for everyone. In the beginning, COVID isolated us like we had never known. It was strange. It was relaxing. It was uncomfortable. It offered time for self-reflection. It was lonely. And this uncertain journey continues.

Many people still are confused by that beastly "Now what?" Our work lives have been dramatically altered. Our social lives are beginning to return to normal—yet "normal" is different.

Many people are struggling with the balance between comfortable aloneness and loneliness. *Do I want to be more social? Or do I like staying at home more than I used to? Am I wrong for wanting to be alone?*

With alone time comes that dreaded list of "shoulds." It destroys the comfortable alone time by constantly knocking on our head with all the things we "should" be doing, like socializing more, or connecting to friends and family. Or curing cancer.

For some, *Am I lonely?* is easily translated to *Am I lazy?* or *Am I crazy for feeling lonely and lazy?* And while you're sitting there with nothing to do but create questions: *If I wonder if I'm crazy, lazy, and lonely, does that mean of course I am?*

There is one comforting thought that is absolutely true: you might be alone in your home and your head, but you are absolutely not alone in this feeling! COVID gave this gift to millions. Also, please always remember that there are many, many people out there who would love to help you. That is the absolute truth.

You might feel lonely, but you are never alone.

Let's briefly look at the other side. There are times when being alone is healthy. Again, we all need to occasionally plug in our USB cable and take time to reboot. Many people love solitude. Contrary to what some might think, older adults who are alone several hours every day are often comfortable and content. They have come to a place in life where they appreciate peace. That statement triggers an eye-opening thought. Perhaps the opposite of lonely is peaceful. The desire to be alone does not mean that you are avoiding people. Solitude is healthy. These older adults have become more emotionally comfortable. Emotion and intellect improve when we are alone—through reading, writing, thinking, creating, meditating, or praying.

For younger people to crave more activity and social connections is natural. But in today's world of technology, that craving becomes distorted. Posting on social media and texting are not social connections. A study by the *American Journal of Preventative Medicine* found that young adults who daily spend over two hours on social media are twice as lonely as those who spend thirty minutes.[39]

For all of us, being on our devices can trigger loneliness. As humans, we are designed for in-person connection. Digital connections are often the reverse of connection, and social media can be a huge depressant. Scrolling through others' bragging posts will only throw gasoline on the feeling-lonely fire.

Another aspect of loneliness comes from our family connections. Thirty percent of people who are unhappy in family relationships feel lonely most or all of the time. That might be a call to explore and analyze personal relations and discover what you are missing and where you might find new connections. That requires vulnerability.

Loneliness also doesn't always mean being alone. Sometimes being

39 Brian A. Primack et al., "Social Media Use and Perceived Social Isolation Among Young Adults in the US," *American Journal of Preventive Medicine*, July 1, 2018, https://www.ncbi.nlm.nih.gov/pmc/articles/PMC5722463/.

in a large party or event can feel lonely. To feel isolated while everyone else is connecting and having fun is devastating. And again, COVID has made many feel much more awkward in social situations.

So, what do we do if we're feeling lonely?

One of the keys to combating loneliness is to focus on others' feelings and needs. That is always the beginning of meaningful relations. Simply take your mind off you for a while and help someone else who might also be lonely. Listen and learn. Don't connect on the phone or online. Meet in person. If you're at one of those large events and feeling alone, simply look for someone else who is standing alone or appears frightened. Introduce yourself.

Whatever your loneliness might come from, the solution is just like that of any other mental struggle: small steps. Don't feel like you must take on the world and instantly become Miss Congeniality. Simply take a small step.

Here are a few simple ideas for small steps:

- Call a friend and talk about it.

- Look online for a neighborhood club, organization, or event.

- Check out the many ideas on Meet-Up for social gatherings.

- Research volunteer opportunities.

- Start a game night with two or three friends.

- Explore a new community of people with similar interests, such as reading, cooking, dancing, or other fun ideas.

- Explore sporting events, theater, or festivals.

- Talk to a therapist.

Always remember: what you're hiding is probably one of your biggest strengths.

TAKING A NEW TURN

I'll repeat this line once again: the opposite of almost any struggle is connection. When we develop and nurture our connection to other human beings, we greatly improve our chances of resilience. Believe it or not, people who die early are often defined as quiet, polite, "well behaved," and passive. When we openly share our pain and suffering with others, we begin to see that we are not alone and that others want to help us. That fuels a longer life, and a richer one.

Four factors are suggested to assist in promoting a longer, and happier life.[40]

The first is to share your distress and concerns with others, as I just mentioned. Find a community and talk to people. Build new friendships.

The second factor is to have goals and commitments. The goals should include others—in other words, being of service and allowing your talents to help other people. The longest-lived survivors are often those who help others survive.

Number three is trying to maintain a positive attitude. Helping others and being of service is a great medication to avoid sadness and loneliness.

The last factor contributing to longer survival is of course physical activity. Not only will having a regimen of exercise help your body, but it is the number one recommended treatment for depression as well.

One thing in life we can always change is our perspective. It sounds so shallow to simply say, "Just think happy," but that is the key to being happy. I keep mentioning that clinical depression is real. It is a chemical imbalance in our brains. Perhaps medication is necessary. However, for many people, the problem is simply negative and critical thinking

---

40 Jill Suttie, PhD, "Four Keys to Well-Being that May Help You Live Longer," Greater Good Magazine, April 13, 2022.

about the world, about others, and about what "might" happen.

I will also mention again that today's social media does not help. Perhaps that might be step one: to switch your social media to only the positive sites. Better yet, exercise, talk to others, build a community, and begin to help the world.

An ancient sacred teacher, Fazang (Fa-Tsang 643–712), once said that emptiness is the same as fullness, just seen from a different perspective.[41] We say that the coffee cup is empty; but empty means filled with space, filled with possibilities, ready for anything. Every moment of time, every point in space, is completely empty, and completely open for what wants to come.[42]

Empty is always ascribed a negative meaning. "My soul feels empty." An optimist looks at empty as opportunity. "My life is empty" means that I am free to go in any direction, with unlimited possibilities.

Your mind is the window to the world. All windows get a little foggy when the road is not clear up ahead. Have faith that the fog will clear and your mind will again see your future clearly.

Everything is uncertain except faith, love, and hope. The medication for uncertainty is hope.

"I'VE JUST ALWAYS DONE IT THAT WAY."

Are you someone who resists change, or do you love change and progress? Seriously contemplate that question. It could be vital to your future.

Life is change. To live is to constantly deal with change—or, even better, create change.

A Lincoln Financial Group ad states: "Do something big while there's still time to put it in your autobiography."

---

41 Fazang, a leading figure of medieval Chinese Buddhism, 643–712 CE.

42 Stephen Mitchell, *The Enlightened Mind* (New York, NY: HarperPerennial, 1991).

Change can begin with a simple shift in our routines. Add something new to your to-do list today—something you have never tried, explored, read about, or considered.

Are there areas of your routines that no longer fit you? Why do you still live in those routines? There are many ways to change routines, but you first must decide *why* you want to change them. Perhaps they are now affecting your life in a negative way. Do they negatively affect others' lives? Perhaps they are simply routine, and you haven't even thought about them.

Then there are exciting reasons to change routines. How can change make life more exciting? Routines might be working just fine, but a shift could make life fun for a change. You'll never know unless you try. The older you get, the more you realize that *fun is important!* You've earned it.

THE MENTAL GYM
Start a Group

I have always had fun starting many different kinds of groups: a brainstorming group for marketing ideas; an early-morning breakfast for interns in entertainment; game night for new friends; Sunday brunches for other MFT therapists.

Come up with a clever name for the group. For instance, the group I started for therapists is called Shrink Outside the Box.

Your group can be for support, having fun, raising money, or all of the above. I usually come up with a theme each time we meet, a topic to discuss, or an assignment to bring an object, like a favorite family photo. Writing groups are always exciting. You can write during the group or come with a previously written assignment. Book clubs are also stimulating.

A Tibetan theory teaches us that one of the most powerful methods of healing is based on compassion, i.e., "the wish to free other beings from their suffering."[43] Just the thought of compassion will shift our thinking away from our own suffering and toward the realization that "the ultimate purpose of our life is to be of benefit to others." Thus a group can assist in solving your hurdles as well as helping others. You never know when a friend might be feeling lonely. Your call to invite her to game night could completely change her mood.

A few times when I have started groups, I have brought several old, silly hats or wigs, and each person draws a number and has to wear that wig or hat during the group. It adds a whole new spark to the conversation. What could be better to post on Facebook than a group photo of that?

Many thanks to Brian, Danny, and Peter for Yada-Yada Sisterhood. Here are some basic steps to follow in this exercise:

- Begin a group for a weekly discussion of moving forward in life.

- Create questions to ask each other:

- What might I become?

- As a child, what did I want to be when I grew up?

- Why didn't I become that? (Or maybe I did, and now I'm no longer happy.)

- If I could do anything, what would it be?

- Ask the group to each bring a friend. And speaking of friends, dig up old friends you haven't spoken to in a long while and start a group with them. Bringing your past with you will create your future.

- Start a gratitude group. Choose four or five good friends and ask them to email their morning gratitude list to each other.

43 Pende Hawter, Buddhist monk, founder of Karuna; *Healing: A Tibetan Buddhist Perspective*, www.buddhanet.net/tib_heal.htm, 1995.

It can be a beautiful way to begin the day, searching for the positive. Write just three things you are grateful for, or three things that happened the day before. It might be a realization, a simple thought, a discovery, or something small like a bird or flower or taste.

A MINDFUL MOMENT

Begin with your deep breathing. This time, as you take in the first breath for four seconds, say to yourself, "One breath." As you hold the breath, say, "One minute." As you release the breath, say, "One hour."

On the second breath in, say, "One day." Hold it and say, "One week." Release it and say, "One month." Breath in for the third time and say, "One year." Hold: "One life." Release: "One universe."

Your breath is only a very short moment in the entire history of the universe. Millions of people have been breathing for millions of years. This one breath is your current moment in time, one tiny moment of your life. Hold it, and then release it to the unknown universe. Contemplate the contrast, as well as the unity, of this breath with the past and future of the universe.

Slowly begin to hum. Don't have any particular song in mind. Just hum.

CHAPTER 9

Am I Really Forking Happy?

"SWEET" SUCCESS

When I was in seventh grade, I had to write a paper about success. My title was "Success is Simply Happiness." When I told that to my father at the dinner table on the night before the paper was due, he put down his fork, looked directly at me, and said, "All of my buddies in World War II did not die happy. Are you telling me they were not successful?" In my mind, I thought about changing the title to "Just Don't Die," but instead I sat in silence with the rest of my siblings, knowing this moment definitely was not happy, and thus neither my title nor my paper were a success.

I think possibly what I learned from that dinner is that success does not equal happiness, nor does happiness mean success.

Ever since then, the definition of success has been on my mind. While I was a reporter for the student paper in college, I wrote an article about "What Is Success?" I interviewed several students, and most of them had my early-childhood definition: happiness. So I would ask them, "Are you happy when you're studying?" "Are you happy when negative circumstances happen that eventually bring success?" The unanimous answer was "Hmmm."

Our mayor at the time in Cincinnati was Jerry Springer. He was also our commencement speaker. I had an interview scheduled with him on the day of homecoming, and I was excited to ask him how he defined success. When we got together, he asked if we could come back and do the interview later because he had an urgent meeting to attend. I am ashamed to say I went back to the fraternity, got drunk, and missed our interview. C'mon. It was homecoming! Needless to say, it was not a successful day.

So, what is success? That is one of the most beautiful explorations each individual can make. The dictionary defines it as "the accomplishment of an aim or purpose." Thus, each person must recognize his/her own goal and purpose. Once again, as I have said so many times throughout this book, the journey is the destination. The questions are the journey. Goals change. They might be achieved, discarded, or interrupted. The blessing is that new goals are always waiting.

Perhaps success is no regrets. It will be determined on our deathbeds. Success for me is learning—not necessarily achieving, but making an attempt and learning. Success is continuing the journey. It will only be achieved when we die. Ironically, my thought about changing the title of my seventh-grade paper to "Just Don't Die" was close; it should have been "Just Wait Till You Die." Or possibly the title should have been "Keep Your Fork."

Success blooms from failure along that journey.

KNOCKING THE *F* OUT OF FAILURE

"Learn to fail, or fail to learn." —Thomas Edison

There is a huge difference between failing and being a failure. Ironically, failing makes you less of a failure. You can only grow from failing. If you're not willing to fail, you cannot innovate and make change. If you don't step through the uncertainty of making an attempt, you will never achieve success.

Failure and success lie in exactly the same direction. That is why the journey is the reward and success lies in taking the journey, not the end result.

I did not believe I had any chance of achieving a master's degree. Every fear from my life came screaming forward. I was not smart enough. I was too old. I had never been a good reader, and chemotherapy dramatically changed my ability to recall what I read. However, if I truly believed that success is making the attempt and "learning," I had to try. Simply deciding to try would be a successful feat.

After stepping through the fear, I told myself that sitting in a classroom couldn't be any worse than sitting in a chemotherapy transfusion room—or worse yet, sitting alone in the regret that I never tried.

I applied for a master's in clinical psychology, with a specialty in LGBTQ studies that would require two additional quarters. I was accepted and began the journey just three months after the day at the beach when I called my sister in desperation. I cried on the first day of school when our first assigned book was Viktor Frankl's *Man's Search for Meaning*. I had just finished reading it, and it was probably the most influential lesson of my journey. I took that as a sign.

Following that book were dozens of others. I read them all. I still have every book on a bookshelf so that I can stare at them in disbelief that I read every single one of them.

The fear of underachieving slowly dissolved as I recognized the power of my life experiences when it comes to genuine psychology. Being the oldest in the class was often a blessing (and a curse) as the teachers would ask me for my advice. We all remember those dreadful days when our grandfathers would say, "I'll tell you what it was like when . . ." I often felt like Grandpa.

This grandpa was selected to be commencement speaker when I graduated. In front of thousands, I spoke through tears as I explained that psyche means "soul," and psychology is the study of the soul. We can't study it until we begin to explore our own soul. So many of my classmates had exposed their souls as a means of learning to help others. Perhaps success is simply exploring our soul.

SO THEN, DAD, IF SUCCESS ISN'T HAPPINESS, WHAT IS HAPPINESS?

Happiness is different than humor. Humor is laughter in the moment, and although happiness is also appreciated in the moment, it is more long term and goes to the core of who we are. It exists much deeper in our soul.

One huge factor in happiness during my cancer journey was literally researching happiness. That research continued during my education. I read books and articles about it, and I started my own exploration with friends and family, asking what makes them happy. Almost every answer was simple, and it always involved others. Their happiness came from helping and being helped and loved. I received a beautiful poem from my cousin, Mary C. It was titled "YOU make me happy." In the poem, "you" refers to everyone in her world.

I questioned and researched why there aren't college classes for "Happiness 101." Turns out, happiness is becoming one of the most popular courses of study in universities, generally titled positive psychology. Study after study has shown that older people are happier people. That includes studies from the CDC and several Gallup Polls.[44] Contrary to the common belief that young people have all the fun and aging makes us sad, self-loathing, and lonely, the results reveal the opposite to be true.

What makes older people happier and better workers? Obviously they have more experience and knowledge, but they have also learned to engage more comfortably with their emotions, such as fear, self-criticism, and sadness. They develop compassion and lose despair. In other words, they become better able to interpret, process, and let go of difficult emotions. Laura Carstensen, a psychologist and director of the

---

44 Centers for Disease Control and Prevention, "Well-Being Concepts," https://www. cdc.gov/hrqol/wellbeing.html; Gallup World Poll, Global Happiness Center, *World Happiness Report*, 2022.

Stanford Center of Longevity, explained in detail in her TEDxWomen Talk that this phenomenon is not generational. In other words, it is not extant only in this currently aging baby boomer generation. It is a human evolution. Once our brains mature enough to recognize that we won't live forever, we inherently choose to live fuller lives. We see priorities more clearly, and we invest in more positive emotions.[45]

There is such irony in the common belief that we will be miserable in old age. Maybe all it takes to dispel this myth is a phone call to Grandma.

Another reason older people are happier is because they have overcome more difficulties in life. Challenges make us happy. Not gifts. Challenges. When we work through something difficult, we discover true happiness. It can't be handed to us in a lottery ticket. Sorry to disappoint you.

As we age, we worry more and more about health and wealth. We worry that we'll be sick or poor. Ironically, as we get to the points in our lives when that might happen, we have learned to not sweat the small stuff or worry about what "might" happen. Let your kids do the worrying.

As Mark Twain said so brilliantly: "Age is an issue of mind over matter. If you don't mind, it doesn't matter."

Money and health are not the keys to happiness. As I have mentioned in so many areas of this book, true joy comes from community. Honest human connection is having friends to talk to, to laugh with, and to cry with.

There are now more Americans over the age of sixty than under the age of fifteen. We have a generation that has the ability, and I might add duty, to develop a new culture of more positivity. Most organizations remain handicapped by the old attitudes and beliefs that younger

---

45 Laura Carstensen, Psychologist, Director of Stanford Center of Longevity, *What Makes Older People Happier?*, (TEDxWomen, 2011).

workers are more motivated, happy, and better workers. Almost every fact would prove that wrong. Because of that misconception, older workers often pursue their dreams independently instead of handing their precious time to a company that won't value them.

If you're a corporation that is hiring, consider the number of nights an older person might stay out partying, or the number of months she takes off for maternity leave. Just sayin'. Now, granted, they might have a few more doctor visits, and they might get lost in the hallways, but God love 'em, they're happy.

The greatest beauty of happiness is that we cannot always plan it. Imagine if you won the lottery. Sounds like a beautiful gift. Then imagine that it destroys your marriage and your entire personal world. Believe it or not, people who have survived cancer are much happier than people who won the lottery.[46] Cancer survivors learn to discover and accept love, appreciate life, and find purpose. They often find a new value to life. As mentioned above, they find happiness in overcoming a difficult challenge.

Lottery winners very often lose everything that cancer survivors discover.

Another misconception about happiness is the belief that it results from material pleasures, power, money, or fame. Taking into consideration, as I mentioned, that happiness actually exists in the present moment, if we are concentrating on what we don't have and so desperately crave, we put ourselves into a state of unhappiness. This is not to imply at all that rich, famous, powerful people cannot be happy. Also, sometimes the striving and hard work can make us happy. Rewards can generate happiness. The answer lies in discovering whether you feel excited by opportunity or saddened by jealousy and envy.

46 Stephen Hall, "The Cancer Lottery," *MIT Technology Review*, December 12, 2016, https://www.technologyreview.com/2016/12/12/69360/the-cancer-lottery/.

The greater the level of calm in our mind and the greater our peace of mind, the greater our ability to enjoy a happy and joyful life.

As was discussed in the last chapter, our feelings of contentment are strongly influenced by our tendency to compare. Who is smarter, more beautiful, or more successful? Once our basic needs are met, we don't need more money, we don't need to have a perfect body, we don't need fame—right now, *at this very moment*, we have our minds and our hearts, which are all the basic equipment we need for happiness.

You can wait for all the good stuff to happen, and then be happy. Or you can be happy, and all the good stuff will happen.

It is also important to be conscious of the emotional state of those with whom you choose to share your personal life. Psychiatrist Irvin Yalom says that people who feel empty never heal by merging with another incomplete person.[47] Sometimes in life, we need to step away from a family member or friend. If interacting with them is making you unhappy, examine your part in the relationship, and then decide the healthy move forward.

The Institute for Brain Potential in Los Banos, California, has determined several interesting and pertinent statistics around happiness. According to their research, 50 percent comes from genetics, and 40 percent comes from intentional activity. That is the part we can alter. The remaining 10 percent comes from happy circumstances that simply occur in our lives.[48]

As I mentioned before, money only brings happiness to the extent that it alleviates poverty. Beyond that, it does little to increase sustained

[47] Irvin D. Yalom, *Love's Executioner* (New York, NY: HarperCollins, Harper-Perennial, 1990).

[48] Brian E. King, PhD, Institute for Brain Potential, *The Habits of Happy People* (Los Banos, CA, 2014).

happiness. Since 1950, our level of wealth in America has doubled, and yet we are less happy.

The purpose of our existence is to seek happiness. It is not self-centered or self-indulgent to constantly be on that search. Happy people are generally more sociable, flexible, and creative. And most important, happy people are found to be more loving and forgiving. They maintain a quality of openness and willingness to reach out to others.

What about happiness in the workplace? For most people, our workplace takes up a huge percentage of our existence.

Dr. Aymee Coget teaches happiness. She is basically a happiness doctor. Literally, she has a PhD in happiness. What she teaches her students and audiences is empowerment, resiliency, and contentment. One of her main teachings might sound surprising: Salary is not an indicator of happiness. Nor is happiness related to time off, lunches, or vacations. Instead, happiness comes from feeling valued and utilizing your strengths.[49] Bosses should learn gratitude and exhibit it among their workers. Employees who work in a loving and caring culture report higher levels of satisfaction and teamwork. In other words, they are happy.[50]

Ask yourself this question: if you are not happy at work, what percentage of your salary would you be willing to give up to be happier?

AND MOST OF ALL, KINDNESS

The reward to living is giving. If you keep your fork and dessert arrives, share the sweetness.

Absolutely nothing brings us joy more than helping others. It is

49 Aymee Coget, PhD, *Happiness for Humankind Playbook; Sustainable Happiness in 5 Steps,* 2020.

50 Barbara Bry and Neil Sentura, "Investing in Happiness A Profitable Pursuit," *San Diego Union-Tribune,* January 5, 2015.

so important to remember the joy that will fill our hearts when we do a kind gesture for someone else. I have shared many stories of people helping me throughout my life, and they are some of my most powerful memories.

There are so many simple ways to help others. On a daily basis, most of us interact with the homeless. We can ignore their requests, we can be angry that this situation exists, or we can be judgmental in our belief that they should "just get a job."

Or we could simply say hello and smile, and ask their name. They are human beings with much bigger challenges than most of us.

When was the last time you were on an elevator and complimented a stranger? Not long ago, I was on an elevator alone when the door opened and a woman entered. I told her she looked so beautiful. Then I noticed she seemed a little uncomfortable. I immediately cried, "I'm gay! Please don't be afraid."

I've also learned that one of the best compliments is when you see someone being a great parent. Just telling them that you observed how much love they give their child is so rewarding. They will often cry. Then I cry. I will add that I have sadly learned you can't say anything to the child. It must be to the parent. Otherwise, it crosses the "creepy" line.

Compliment cashiers, mailmen, doormen, baristas, or garbage workers. The list is endless. It will always make their day. I mentioned earlier that, as a great boss, Mitt Romney taught us that every single person's job is just as important as anyone else's. Just say, "Thank you. I appreciate you."

SO, TO RECAP HAPPY

Calmer people are happier.

Relax. You can't be told how to be happy. Each person derives happiness in a unique manner from the inside. It must be personally discovered, or else it isn't making you truly happy.

A woman told me in a session one time that she was sick and tired of people telling her to be happy. "I don't want to be happy! I want to be proud. I want to be liked. I want to be a good person. But I don't want to be all mushy-gushy happy." By the end of the conversation, which was a discussion about her success at being proud, liked, and good, she admitted that she had definitely achieved all of those attributes. When asked if that made her happy, she said, "Okay. I'm fucking happy. I just don't like admitting it."

Was she happy or not?

I think the moral of that story is that happiness is not always displayed on the outside and not always labeled with the *H*-word. Does it matter? If you're just content, are you happy?

If helping others makes us happy, which it almost always does, then be happy without being discouraged that you possibly didn't make the receiver happy. Your happiness is not dependent on others' happiness.

I saw a homeless woman on the street in San Francisco one day. I thought I would surprise her, so I went into a restaurant and ordered a club sandwich. As I handed it to her, in all of my excitement, she said, "You could have asked me if I was a vegetarian first." Quite honestly, that response made me even happier in the moment. She wasn't happy.

Happiness can be generated through the expressions of positive emotions. Express gratitude. When making a gratitude list, what makes us happy is not what we are writing on the list but rather the physical intention of thinking, contemplating, and reading it. What makes us happy is wanting to make ourselves happy. Another form of happiness comes from knowing we are loved and then expressing that love and gratitude to those people.

We get happier as we get older. We slowly learn "that shit" doesn't matter.

These are the happiest groups of people:

1. Women more than men
2. People over sixty
3. Parents

Stress is the biggest enemy of happiness. It is impossible to be stressed and happy at the same time. Stress is the feeling of lost control. The key to reducing stress is to feel a sense of control over the stressor, which we can achieve through perspective. It is helpful to record our immediate responses. What are our automatic thoughts when a stressor occurs? Mindfulness can assist in habitual expression—moment-to-moment awareness to discourage undesirable habits.

I was recently in a Starbucks, and an elderly man was ahead of me in line. I became so angry and judgmental as he kept trying to pay with the app on his cell phone and it wasn't working. Just as I was reaching my peak of anger, he turned around and said to me, "I remember the days when 'pay phones' were so heavy you couldn't even carry them."

I laughed so hard and learned that my anger could be immediately reversed with a little humor from a happy old man. (He was happy. Not "app-y.")

Happy people are more successful.

Again, money can't buy happiness, but happiness can buy money.

There, Dad! I finally answered the friggin' question. Exactly fifty years later. Success doesn't mean happy. Maybe happy becomes success.

And scene.

SIX KEY ELEMENTS TO BEING HAPPY

They have been worded in many ways, on many lists, and by many happy (and unhappy) people, but they all contain the same basic six categories:

1. *Be grateful and express your gratitude.* "When you appreciate what you have, what you have appreciates in value."[51] There is an important introspective rule in this category. If we are not happy with what we currently have, the odds are fairly high that we will not ever be happy with what we have. "I'll be happy if I get *x*" is not living in the moment, on your path, and for yourself.

2. *Be kind.* Selflessly and anonymously helping another human being is an excellent way to feel good inside by releasing serotonin in your brain. It is physically and emotionally rewarding. By anonymous, I don't necessarily mean that you cannot tell someone. I mean that you do it in a humble, sincere, and caring manner, rather than to bring attention and acclaim to yourself.

3. *Forgive.* As I have mentioned, living with resentment is like taking poison and hoping the other person dies. You are the only one suffering. Let it go. From that nasty driver on the freeway this morning to your first-grade teacher who ridiculed you in front of the class, make a choice to completely forget it. Do you think they remember? Forgiveness is for you! For-you-giveness.

4. *Relish joy.* True happiness will occur when you slow your life, even for a moment, and enjoy joy. Do not rob yourself of the happiness. Cherish these times when they happen and mark them in your mind. Remember these moments instead of the resentments. Look for what I like to call "MOPs": moments of perfection. They occur when you see the perfect sunrise, or find yourself eye-to-eye with a bunny rabbit, or amid that first bite of ice cream. I think of it every morning with my first sip of coffee.

---

51 Jacob Sokol, life and leadership coach, founder of Sensophy Life Coaching, Brooklyn, New York, https://www.sensophy.com.

5. *Connect with a larger power.* Whether you are spiritual or not, allow yourself the comfort of knowing that the entire universe does not center around you. There are many things bigger than you. Even if it is simply the connection between everything that exists, there is a force and a source to all that is around us. We all have moments when we feel that everything is completely connected at that instant. We are at peace. Everything is right. That is the connection.

6. *Exercise.* Taking care of your body will only heighten your happiness. It allows you to tap into your endorphins, just as you do through love, kindness, and yes, an orgasm. No matter what your level of physical ability, you can almost always do something to elevate your energy, which improves your mental and emotional levels. Consistent exercise has been proven to raise happiness levels in people with clinical depression.

Many people might think of death as the end of happiness or "losing the battle." I believe heaven is the ultimate party, so why wouldn't I want to get there? I always joke with my friends that life on earth is just a stop at 7-Eleven on the way to the party. I definitely want to get my chips and beer and get to the party, but meanwhile, I'm enjoying the Slurpees and crazy people.

UNHAPPY VS. HAPPY

"Okay," says Debbie Downer, "so then how do I know if I am really happy or not? What's the definition of unhappy?"

These are a few characteristics of unhappy people:
- Judgment and jealousy of others
- Inability to accept life and relinquish control when necessary
- Negative outlook on the future
- Making excuses

- Lack of trust
- Dwelling in the current struggles
- Stressing over the what-ifs
- Complaining, whining, gossiping, and ridiculing

The difference between happy and unhappy people is essentially the amount of time we stay attached to our bad events. In no way does that mean "just get over it." As I have mentioned several times, a period of grieving and pain is vital when something traumatic has happened. The goal is to eventually rediscover happiness.

So much of our unhappiness is buried deep inside our childhood and/or our culture. We learn our belief system from our parents, religion, grandparents, teachers, television, and friends.

For instance, my grandmother always said that God loves the poor. Little Billy heard, "God hates the rich." I still have to fight that instinctual belief that all poor people are going to heaven and all rich people are already in hell just for being able to shop at Versace.

Money has zero to do with being good or evil, and as I mentioned earlier, once we have enough to survive, money has no effect on our ability to be happy.

Happier people tend to look at life with curiosity rather than victimhood. Instead of complaining constantly, they devote that time to problem-solving. They are goal oriented and focused. Happier people see others as good, and they believe in the goodness of humanity. They accept others with an open heart. They recognize that just because *you* have money, luck, and good fortune does not mean that *they* cannot have it as well. There is not a limited amount of good.

Happier people let shit happen. They tend to roll with the punches rather than spin in the fear. Fall down. Get up. Rinse and repeat.

How do we shift our brains from unhappy to happy? First of all, just like relaxation simply involves the release of all effort, optimism is a natural state that our brains crave. Please let that sink in. We crave happiness, just like food. Optimism begins with the release of bad emotions. Inside all of us, we harbor courage, faith, honesty, love, perseverance, knowledge, and hope.

There are known methods to help our brains become more positive. I mentioned at the beginning of chapter 6 that in CBT (cognitive behavioral therapy), the theory is that you can teach yourself to be aware of your negative thoughts. Stop them, change them, and release them; you can begin immediately. When you just read that sentence, did you think, *What bullshit—that's easy to say*? Be aware that you just thought that. How might you reword it?

Right now, stop being angry. Release it. Instead, ask yourself what it would look like if you had no anger. It serves no purpose. Fear, when we embrace it, can at least motivate us. Anger is poison. As I mentioned, most anger is based in fear, so go deeper than the anger and ask yourself what you fear.

Ask yourself, *What can I feel instead? What would bring me hope? What is out there for me to learn?* Thinking about what could bring hope brings hope. Thinking about what might make you happy will make you happy. It is that simple. You cannot think happy thoughts and be sad or angry at the same time.

You might truly be "keeping your fork" and believe that something sweet is coming, but you have to read the menu first. If you say no to dessert, you won't get it. So start exploring the opportunities.

Ask yourself, *When have I been most happy?* Ponder that question for a while. Why were you happy at that point in your life?

We can often find happiness in basic planning. It may not go as we hope, but we can enjoy the moment of planning. Make plans. Write endless "to-do" lists. It's helpful. Being productive is a positive feeling. You will never know the outcome, but you can certainly have tremendous input in the journey. And while you're making lists, don't forget to make a list of everyone you love. Don't forget the list of everyone who loves you. Love exists in the present moment. Appreciate it and express it.

What lights your fire, floats your boat, puts a little shimmy in your shamrock? What fills your fork?

If you are dealing with a loss, it is not possible for life to be the same again, so it's important to discover and embrace a new future. Please allow time. Grief is a long and necessary process. Embrace the love that causes the grief.

Eliminating the things in our lives that lead to suffering is not an easy task, but as we clean that closet, we can find joy and excitement in accumulating new things that will lead us to happiness. The process starts with slowly increasing our awareness of what makes us unhappy. That is important before attempting to discover what makes us happy.

I recently found several poems that I wrote between ages six and nine. It can't be a coincidence that every one of them contains the word *gay*. That was not the word used for homosexuality back then; it was a description I used for happy people. These are a few excerpts:

It was a Spring day
Nice and sunny
Mr. Squirrel was out
And Mrs. Bunny

All the children were out to play
All so happy
All so gay

———————————

A day in February
When everyone is gay

A day in February
A very special day

Of course it is Saint Valentine
A saint that we all know
He praised, loved, and prayed to God
To him the graces flow.

_____

This Christmas poem
So short and brief
Is so so cheerful and gay
For Christ was born
Many years ago
And He was just that way

AND THEN THERE'S H-U-M-O-R

I can honestly and confidently write this segment about the healing power of humor because I proved it.

I still have three large binders from my cancer journey, titled *Lymph Notes*, and they are filled with funny quotes, stories, and pictures. That was also the title of my blog, which was a great platform for me to put my humor out in the world. I got so much joy in reading the responses from others who shared the laughter.

Humor has always been a big part of my life. When I was a little boy, my father told me that God gave me the gift to laugh, and I should always remember to spread it to others. However, as anyone who knows me will say, I have always been a little twisted with a very sick sense of humor. Dark Irish humor. Things that make me laugh will often horrify others. During my cancer, I made very inappropriate jokes about it. As long as it's *my* cancer, that is fine, but when working with others who have cancer, I often have to bite my tongue.

As I mentioned, humor is different from happy. Happy people don't necessarily laugh all the time, and it is extremely common for funny people to not be happy. Many years ago, someone told me to think of the funniest person I knew. Then they said, "They are probably the saddest person you know, too." That shocked me, but comedians are likely to suffer from anxiety and depression. Sadly, Robin Williams was a perfect example.

Comedians I have seen in my practice have explained that humor was always their means of finding strength to defend and protect the very sad affliction of depression.

Victor Frankl believed that humor is a weapon for our souls to generate self-preservation. According to him, "It is well known that humor, more than anything else in the human make-up, can afford an aloofness and an ability to rise above any situation."[52]

Seeking humor is important. First discover what makes you laugh, and then search for that humor. What is your favorite joke? If you don't have one, then find that perfect standby joke for when someone says, "Tell me a joke." Search for the best one. Don't forget it.

I keep a list of my favorite funny quotes. I pull out the list when I need to smile. Here are a few:

- When my nephew was young, my sister asked him the name of Jesus's father. He responded, "Verge." "Verge?" my sister asked. "Yeah. My teacher keeps talking about Verge 'n Mary."

- Oscar Wilde once said, "Try everything once, except incest and folk dancing."

---

[52] Viktor E. Frankl, *Man's Search For Meaning* (Boston, MA: Beacon Press, 1959).

- I was talking to my sister Kathy one time about how clean she is around her house. She casually said, "Yeah, I'm so anal, it hurts."

- There are three stages of aging: youth, middle age, and "You look good."

And a few of my favorite anonymous quotes:

- "Veni, Vedi, Visa—I came, I saw, I did a little shopping."

- "I killed an ant in my kitchen last week. Now none of my relatives will come visit."

- "What if the Hokey Pokey is really what it's all about?"

- "Time flies like an arrow. Fruit flies like a banana."

- Nothing outside of us will heal us. (Unless we need an organ transplant.)

One of the best lines ever is from my favorite comedian, Demetri Martin: "'I'm sorry' and 'I apologize' are the same thing . . . . unless you're at a funeral."

I have many pages of the funniest lines I have heard in AA meetings and, even funnier, the lines from the readings that have been misread. One of my favorites was the misreading of the phrase "The answers will come if your own house is in order." The shy young newcomer accidently read, "The answers will come if you own a house."

Sing. Dance. Laugh. Play games. Tell jokes. Take risks.

A few years ago, my brother and sister ("the twins") were visiting me in Los Angeles, so I took them to stroll along Rodeo Drive in Beverly Hills. We drifted into Williams Sonoma where we were greeted by an employee who quickly asked, "Where are you from?" She said it in a condescending manner, as if we were fresh off the country farm wagon.

My sister told her we were from Ohio, to which she replied, "That's sweet."

Later, while we were looking at a chicken roasting oven, she came over and asked us if we were interested in learning more about it. My brother conjured up a fake Southern accent and replied, "Nah. In Ohio we just shove a beer can up its ass and throw it on the fire."

THE MENTAL GYM

Humor

If you don't already have a favorite joke, *find one*! Whenever you are at a party or work meeting, you can always bring humor to the table with a great joke.

Document the times in your life when you have laughed the hardest. There are many for me, but I particularly remember the 1980s when I traveled often with my good friends Bill and Glen—joyful spirits who could always make me laugh. We were in Santa Fe one winter, and Bill did his famous "tight-butt walk." I was laughing so hard that I fell on the ice and they had to drag me out of the oncoming traffic. I still have in my will that Bill will do the tight-butt walk at my funeral so I can laugh one more time.

RESEARCH YOUR FUTURE

There are many small steps you can take to contemplate your future. If you sit and think (or lie in the grass and stare at the clouds), you will come up with questions.

These are just a few:

- Ask just one friend to lunch. Have three questions for him/her, such as "What am I good at?" "What might you think would be a good future for me?" "What am I doing wrong in my life right now?"

- Research someone who is doing what you think might be fulfilling for you. Send him/her an email. Spend a day with them at work.

- Without any intent or goal, just start browsing the web. See where you go. What are the first words you will Google?

- Make time for something happy every day. Don't wait for it to happen. Specifically plan something that will make you happy today. Pleasure can become a habit. Your emotions will change. You will see improvement in your mood, self-esteem, and in your hope. I recognize how Pollyanna-ish that might sound: "Just be happy and you'll be happier." It's not rocket science. Until you make the decision to try, you will never know if allowing yourself to be happy makes you happy.

- In your early life, what did you assume would be your future?

- What from your past would you like to bring into your present or future?

- Consciously cultivate gratitude.

- Discover your signature strengths. (You might be very surprised.)

- List your perfect work scenario. Who are you working with? What is the setting? How much are you making? What might you be doing? Believe it!

- Write down your goals and email them to a friend.

- And most importantly, hypothetically figure out how to have everything you want.

A MINDFUL MOMENT

Sit quietly with a friend or loved one. Hold hands. Stare into each other's eyes silently. Guide your friend through the four deep breaths. Four seconds in, hold for four seconds, and four seconds out.

Once completely relaxed and comfortable, begin to ask each other questions . . . without speaking. Do not have the questions planned. Just let them flow naturally. Then allow the other person's eyes to answer the questions silently.

Perhaps the question might be "What is my future?"

When finished, tell that friend your joke.

CHAPTER 10

Resilience IN Purpose
(the RIP before the other RIP)

Whatever your main course that was taken away, you have been handed this transition for a reason. The doubt, the fear, and the uncertainty are sitting on your empty plate for a reason. You have been given the gift of being in this beautiful space that will allow you to process a new, advanced level of living your life. It was given to you to promote change for an intended new future. What will it be? That is the enormous question.

You can't Google the answer. You can't ask a friend. You must live in the process and discover the purpose. I will change that statement. You "get to" live in the process, and you "get to" live a new purpose.

So many times throughout the book I have talked about leaving our comfort zone, which begins at birth. It doesn't take much to recognize the gifts that come from all of those forced changes. We were forced to behave, to go to school, to get a job. Those were all natural, expected societal changes. Now you are in a new zone where society doesn't have a demand. You get to decide and choose whatever you like.

How? What? When?

Each time I stepped through a challenge in my life, I lost enormous amounts of "me." On the delicious main-course plate that was being taken away was my identity and my dreams. I had preconceived notions of who I was and who I was becoming. The universe disagreed. It took away my dinner but secretly promised a beautiful dessert, as long as I held on to my fork. As I have mentioned several times before, I had to grieve the loss of my assumed future.

I now shift my thinking. While eating my dinner, I'm much more focused on the excitement for the dessert. I mean that literally and figuratively. I'm not concentrating on the fact that dinner is going to be gone but instead on what lies ahead. I haven't seen the menu yet, so I have no clue of the possibilities. I just have to trust that there will be greater delights than I could ever cook for myself.

Joy will bloom with a search for meaning and purpose.

One of the greatest sources of purpose is having children. Of course, they come with a great deal of stress, fear, guilt, and hard work, but a parent nurtures this beautiful gift to the world and watches it bloom so that it can then continue the purpose. Each child will add new, unique meaning to your purpose. They will create new purpose and surprise you with what continues to bloom. Please embrace that meaning in your life, but remember not to depend on them for your joy. I also recognize that they don't always bloom in the way you expect.

Some of us don't have that beautiful element in our lives. Throughout my life, I have had many people say to me, "You're so lucky. You don't have kids, so you get to x." I agree that I have taken advantage of my freedom and moved, changed careers, traveled, and had fun. However, don't ever underestimate the flip side: "You're so lucky. You have kids, so you get to x." We all are given blessings, and what we do with them is exactly how we discover our meaning and purpose.

No matter what is handed to us, or what happens to us, the true reward comes from asking, "What was the meaning of that in my life?" Isn't that so much more rewarding than sitting in misery and self-pity?

Another part of our purpose is our legacy. I mentioned that I will forever remember my father promoting the word *yes*. It often came tucked in the phrase "git'er done." And his most powerful statement to me, when I was dealing with the fear of moving away from Ohio: "There will always be reasons to stay but much better reasons to move on." Dad brought meaning to himself by giving me that advice. It has given him even more meaning to share it with you.

What wisdom will your children remember? What do you remember that your parents always told you? How are they similar . . . or not? How have you taken what your parents passed to you and changed it in your unique way to pass on to your children?

Every article and research paper I have read on the subject of happiness concludes the same thing: the key to developing the strongest and highest level of happiness comes from having a sense of purpose outside of ourselves—helping others. That means something completely different for every person. It might begin with your children, or it might be completely fulfilled there.

It may not take a crisis. Many of us have a natural craving for purpose as we reach midlife. Dr. James Hollis talks about "when the second half of life begins." When do you know that you are ready to step into your second half of life? This does not necessarily occur at midlife as is commonly thought. According to Dr. Hollis, the first sign comes when you feel dissatisfied by where you are today. You hear a calling from within to discover a more purposeful life. It is a collision of your "false self," which is created from the expectations of others, and your "true self," which is instinctive.[53] Stop for a moment. Think about that. Your false self vs. your true self.

For others, a forced challenge might be the motivation for change. A crisis not only disrupts our lives but also challenges our self-worth and our place in the world. It will force us away from our old beliefs or stigmas and, even better, others' beliefs or stigmas. It can push us into a new way of perceiving ourselves and the world. We hopefully begin to think from our heart. We can learn to listen to our beautiful, instinctive passion for life.

A powerful example of this is my sister Eileen, one of the most

---

[53] James Hollis, PhD, *Finding Meaning in the Second Half of Life* (New York NY: GothamBooks, 2005).

loving people I have in my life. She and her husband, Paul, left Cincinnati and built a beautiful new home up on Lake Erie. It was a perfect place to retire and live the peaceful life they had always imagined. However, life had a different plan.

One of their daughters has had some personal struggles in her life, so Eileen and Paul had to take in her three young boys and care for them. It is not easy to parent while in one's late sixties, but as I said, Eileen is such a loving and caring person that her taking them in was never even in question. Eventually, they had to sell their beautiful new home on the lake and move closer to their daughter so the children could see their mother.

There is not much doubt that Eileen has found her beautiful new purpose in life; however, it is certainly not what she had dreamed of.

THE SEARCH FOR PURPOSE

The obvious question is "How do I start my search?"

We have the choice to sit and dwell on the horrible things that might happen, or we can focus on the infinite opportunities ahead of us. We can think about possible new goals and avenues to achieve them. Meaningful goal pursuit makes us happy. A commitment to those goals, to a religion, to a community, or to work are related to a pursuit of purpose.

> *"The meaning of life is to find your gift. The purpose of life is to give it away."* —Pablo Picasso

Despite the lessons about success I learned from Dad, I still believe that success and happiness go hand in hand. Living a good life, with meaning and purpose geared toward the common good, will bring success, and happiness as a side effect.

Resilience and purpose are the roads to happiness.

The search isn't always a rosy skip over the rainbow. Sometimes our child brain kicks in with "Oh no!" and "I don't know what to do," or "Why am I so lame?" Allow yourself a little peaceful time to acknowledge these questions. Then ask your adult brain to comment on how it might respond. Even better, team up with another adult brain who knows you and loves you. We are only helping others grow when we allow them into our lives to express themselves and shine their light and beauty. We can become comfortable with kindness. Remember that your purpose cannot be just about you.

This process of exploration is the most important and meaningful part of resilience. Resilience is about re-blooming. Nothing blooms without first planting a seed.

Resilience and purpose is not a destination. It is not a monetary goal or a set deadline. Those are for our career brain—our societal brain. Resilience is an ever-changing process.

One of the best questions to begin a search is "What have I not done in my life that I still want to accomplish?" Try writing just four words that describe your hope for your life and your future.

WHAT IF?

As I said before, fear is based on the future. Have hope that the fear will end. Expect that life will get better—better than it has ever been.

Throughout each decade of my life, I have believed I am currently living my best decade. I think the next one will be terrible because I will be old. I thought that in my twenties, in my thirties, in my forties (you get the idea). And yet, each one got better. Why do I continue to think that the next decade will be the worst?

Learn to expect and believe the opposite of what you fear. Change the nervous "What if?" to a "Wow! What if!" Expect the best that could happen. Stop stressing over the what-ifs and appreciate what is.

AUTHENTIC SELF

Throughout the book, I have offered several exercises for discovering yourself, but the first and most important exercise might be to list the characteristics of your true self and your false self. Many websites can give you ideas for words to use, but *Psychology Today* offers seven qualities of "true self."[54]

- Spontaneity
- Reasoning
- Creativity
- Free will
- Discernment
- Love
- Spirituality

Spontaneity is our ability to express ourselves. If you embrace joy, humor, and natural emotions and feelings, you are acting in true spontaneity. Ask yourself, *Am I enthusiastic in my life?* The opening of this book premised a child being born who gets slapped by the doctor and then says, "Now what?" Children are models of spontaneity. They know nothing more than exploration and curiosity. Two of the many lessons we should learn from them are to not be afraid to cry or say what we are afraid of.

Reasoning simply means sound thinking—our ability to explore and be open to awareness.

Creativity comprises becoming aware of something that no one else has yet seen. We have the amazing power to create. We have thoughts,

---

54 John T. Chirban, PhD, "Seven Qualities of True Self: The Essence of Human Being," *Psychology Today*, August 14, 2013.

and thoughts create ideas. We then have the gift of taking ideas and generating skills that then lead to new possibilities. Creativity does not happen without risk.

Free will is explained in the opening of this chapter. We each choose how we want to think. We have that choice.

Discernment is the ability to make that choice between good and bad. We choose moral or evil. We know, we choose, and we act (ideally on the good). Our ability to choose right from wrong begins at a very young age. As children, we begin to learn (and hopefully are taught) kindness, courage, compassion, and honesty. We also learn we can "discern" which direction we want to head. This marks the beginning of our personal connection to humanity.

Love and *spirituality* are natural human cravings. I have discussed them and their importance throughout this entire book. They are both right in front of us when we are ready to define and accept them for ourselves. They are the two greatest fertilizers for our seeds of resilience.

I have said before that I believe our greatest inner craving is for love, second only to food. We are driven by the powerful urge to love and be loved. Love is trust. It is attraction. It is vulnerability. Through that vulnerability comes safety. Love is emotional, spiritual, physical, sacred, and natural. It is our most fulfilling gift and probably our most difficult to achieve. Just like anything else in life, it works when we work for it.

> *One word frees us of all the weight and pain of life: that word is love.*—Sophocles

As we grow, we develop our own unique ways to express our authentic self. We continually discover it and what it means to live it. How do you dance to your own rhythm?

Consider some of these terms:

- Achievement
- Adventure
- Animals
- Approval
- Art
- Caregiving
- Children
- Compassion
- Competition
- Courage
- Creativity
- Dignity
- Exercise
- Family background
- Fairness
- Financial security
- Food
- Humor
- Independence
- Injustice
- Inspiration
- Knowledge
- Leadership
- Management
- Money
- Music
- Organization
- Parenting
- Passion
- Perfection
- Performance
- Pride

- Purpose
- Relationship
- Research
- Science
- Sex
- Social
- Spiritual
- Teaching

Which of these words resonates with your authentic self? Don't think too much. Just choose the words that lead you to your core. These words can be the stepping stones to learning who you are right now and where you would like to move forward. Once you check the words that are authentically you, put them in order of importance.

Which word do you want to focus on first? What do you know in your heart you need to work on? Are you at a point where you recognize a false self? Are you dissatisfied with where you are right now in life?

I sincerely hope that some of the Mental Gyms or Mindfulness Moments have generated creative scenarios to instigate questions that will lead you closer to a more fulfilled life. *Fulfilled: filled full.* That is the goal. However, remember, just like any sport, the part of the game we enjoy most is the *process* of reaching a goal.

One of the most important parts of this journey to discover who you will be is to look back at who you have been. The first Mental Gym in this book was to create your auto-graph, or your life's timeline of ups and downs. Without question, that is the perfect place to begin your search for your future. You can look at that graph and see where, when, and why you were happy, and what made you happy.

I love the Queen Latifah song "I Know Where I'm Going Because I Know Where I've Been." This is just one verse:

There's a cry in the distance

It's a voice that comes from deep within
There's a cry asking why
I pray the answer's up ahead, yeah
'Cause I know where I've been.[55]

Our past was put there to help us figure out our future. What a shame it would be if we ignored it. Perhaps you loved acting as a child. That means you have a gift at something many others are terrified to attempt. You have the ability to stand up in front of a crowd and share your knowledge. Maybe you loved art or writing earlier in life. That is an incredible gift that can be used to convey a message to the world, not only in paint or pencil but in any medium. Creativity is one of the most profound gifts, capable of idea generating, and not just for you. Think of how many others you can help to create ideas. Imagine how you might help others by using your creativity.

Personal landmarks from our past are incredibly important. Look at your auto-graph and note your accomplishments, such as people you have dated, career successes, places you have traveled, and prizes you have been awarded. Perhaps you were a sports star in high school or organized a student organization. Maybe you have run a marathon or taken a cruise. Reflect on all of them and put them in order of priorities.

Another possible way to organize your past:

• What I did.
• What I learned.
• What I wish I did.
• What I used to dream about.
• What I dream for now.

Another excellent exercise is to design the next year . . . backwards.

---

[55] Produced by Lucian Piane and Marc Shaiman, lyrics by Jason Lynn and Paul Broucek.

What might your perfect life look like in one year? Month by month, write what happened to get there. Start with eleven months from now, then ten, etc.

WAYS TO FIND OUR SOUL

The universe will give us signs of encouragement if we allow ourselves to be aware of them. I'll mention again that synchronicities—strange coincidences that you can't explain but trust are right—are signals that our lives are going in the right direction. This synchronicity is spiritual if you choose to see it that way. So many expressions mark its appearance: "Wow. How did that happen?" "Can you believe that?" And the clearest, most precise example: "WTF?!"

Every spiritual awakening begins with a rude awakening.

What if we shifted our vision in a time of crisis and saw it as an intended synchronicity? What if we began to see life and all of its ups and downs as a plan that was made to help us view ourselves and our world from a different direction? What if our challenges were sent so we can learn to reconnect with our loved ones on a different level? Possibly it is an invitation to turn inwards and reconnect with self. From darkness comes light.

Begin to ask, "Why?" That one incredible word.

We can also designate our own sign connecting us with the universe so that when we see it, we recognize that we are on the right path at that moment. For many people, this sign is something like a butterfly or hummingbird. I have mentioned that for me it is the number 1111. For some Native Americans, it is a feather on the ground in front of you, pointing in the right direction. I have a friend who looks for yellow cars. My friend Bryan was told by his mother on her deathbed that her sign to him will always be a ladybug. Sit quietly, as directed by the Mindful Moment at the end of this chapter, and create your symbol.

Meaning and purpose are based in our spiritual freedom. Spiritual freedom comes from an awakening in our minds. Again, please do not be frightened of the word *spirituality*. Each person defines the level "God" plays in spirituality.

The dictionary has a beautiful definition for spirit: the vital principle in humans, animating the body or mediating between body and soul. *Between body and soul.* Both are wholeheartedly felt. Your body can be touched, broken, and repaired, just like your soul. Your spirit is the mediator between them.

What gets you out of bed in the morning? What motivates you to help another human? What is that amazing feeling you can't explain when you look at your young child? Animated! In many ways, your spirit motivates and animates your body.

What is soul? It's easy to recognize soul in artists and musicians. Not only do they feel compelled to release their talent and expression, but others are moved by the reflection of their soul. Many of us do not have the gift to create music, but we feel the incredible connection to the soul when we hear it. The same is true for art or performance. So many statements express it: "I felt in awe." "I can't explain it." "It brought tears to my eyes." Tears are the number one symbol for feeling your soul. They are your emotions solidified.

What is your history with religion? What is your immediate thought when someone says "God," or "Higher Power"? For many, religion is the basis of a belief system. It is community. It is motivation and purpose. A modern definition of religion is "the subjective experience of a sacred dimension. It is the deepest values and meanings by which to live. It is one's own inner dimension."[56]

For others, spirituality is not about religion but about connecting

---

56 Daphne Rose Kingma, *The Ten Things to Do When Your Life Falls Apart: An Emotional and Spiritual Handbook* (Novato, CA: New World Library, 2010)

to an energy outside of oneself. It is about connecting to the universe. Humility. Finding meaning.

These beliefs can make us strong through any challenge in life.

Finding purpose and discovering a personal meaning can completely change one's perspective when living in fear and hopelessness. We might very well have broken our closest connections when we go through a trauma. Finding something other than ourselves to trust can begin the new journey when we feel like no one can help us. Hope.

Spirituality can also be defined as acceptance. Acceptance of others can be calming and result in greater awareness. Acceptance of yourself and your life as it is at this very moment is as important as acceptance of others. Accept yourself. Be compassionate for your life. And please, more than anything else, accept and respect the beliefs and spirituality of others. Spirituality is beautiful, not competitive.

I was in a small restaurant in Ohio one evening, eating alone and reading a book. At the table next to me were three rowdy children with a young mom. I was in full judgment mode, blaming her for not having more control over the behavior of the children. Mind you, I had no idea of her situation. She could have been a sister, a cousin, a nanny, or any other type of caretaker. I didn't care. It was disturbing *me*!

Several minutes after they left, the waitress came over and told me that the young girl had paid for my meal as an apology. Very quickly, the situation shifted from one filled with anger that I would have forgotten the next morning to a story I will never forget. I went from anger and judgment to gratitude and pure love for her.

Gratitude is spiritual. It shifts our brains into a positive frame of mind and offers the alternative of love. It can turn something simple into something profound. It was amazing to me how quickly this young girl went from a nuisance to the Virgin Mary in my mind. And nothing was different but my point of view—how I chose to narrate the story in my head. To me, that is purely spiritual. Spirituality can simply be a rowdy young family at Skyline Chili.

What if she had not paid for my meal? I still could have easily changed my thoughts. I could have been grateful that those children had a mother. I could have celebrated their loud laughter and excitement. The sounds of children are the sounds of life, like birds or water. I could have contemplated the things that made me laugh as a child. And most of all, I could have paid for their meal! It taught me, loudly and clearly, that small acts of kindness are love, spirit, and purpose. It taught me *so* many things on *so* many levels.

About ten years later, I was alone in a restaurant in Los Angeles, in the exact same scenario of sitting near a young mother with three rowdy children. I did not even hesitate. I hurried and finished my meal, went to the cashier, and paid for their meals. I could finally say thank you to that mother in Ohio.

Holistic author Madisyn Taylor writes that everything in the universe ebbs and flows.[57] It gives and takes, expands and contracts. If we only feel gratitude when it serves our desires, we are not being grateful. Fate may take our possessions, situations, or even people we love. During those times, we struggle to find gratitude, but by holding on to our fork and trusting in hope that we can discover a new level of purpose, we will find a new level of gratitude like we have never known.

There are also proven physical benefits of gratitude. Five minutes a day of gratitude can increase your long-term well-being by more than 10 percent.

Gratitude generates social capital. In other words, it makes people

---

57 Madisyn Taylor, *Unmedicated: The Four Pillars of Natural Awareness* (New York, NY: Atria Books, 2018); "Being Truly Thankful," "Beyond Counting Blessings," Daily-OM.com; https://www.madisyntaylor.com/wp/.

more attracted to us. In two studies, those who were 10 percent more grateful had 17.5 percent more social capital.[58]

The studies also show that gratitude makes us nicer, more trusting, more social, and of course, more appreciative. As a result, it allows us to make more friends and deepen our existing relationships. Surprisingly, keeping a gratitude journal caused participants to report the following:

- 16 percent fewer physical symptoms
- 19 percent more time exercising
- 10 percent less physical pain
- 25 percent increased sleep quality
- 30 percent lowered depressive symptoms

For that, you can be grateful.

Just this moment, as I write the final lines of this book, I see a woman drop a $20 bill. I walk over, touch her on the shoulder, and hand her the money. She hugs me.

A small act that makes me very happy. Spirituality.

I am grateful that I had the opportunity to offer this book to you, and I am immensely grateful that you took the time to read it. I can only hope that it gave you a little hope that something sweet is coming.

THE MENTAL GYM

Answer these three questions:

If you could tell the entire world one message, what would it be? Pretend you have won an Oscar and are standing in front of the

---

[58] Amid Amin, "The 31 Benefits of Gratitude You Didn't Know About: How Gratitude Can Change Your Life," HappierHuman.com, August 1, 2020, https://www.happierhuman.com/benefits-of-gratitude/.

microphone, the entire world waiting for your message. It is criminal to say "I really don't have anything planned" or "I guess I just want to thank my family." As an old entertainment writer, I can tell you that when you thank someone in an acceptance speech, you make one person very happy, and the rest of the world is bored. So, what is the message you would like to convey to everyone?

Secondly, what gift do you think you are meant to give to the world? I don't mean a literal gift, but a trait, a talent, or knowledge.

The third question is what do you still hope the world will give back to you? In other words, what is something you still hope to experience or learn?

A MINDFUL MOMENT
Going Forward, Be Mindful

Mindfulness is an intentional acceptance and nonjudgmental focus of our attention on thoughts, emotions, and sensations occurring in the present moment in our bodies.

"Nonjudgmental" is an important part of that explanation. Our minds will naturally drift away to think about stressors, or dinner, or what the kids are doing. That's okay. Be aware of the drifting and allow your focus to come back to your breathing.

I ended chapter 1 by talking about mindfulness, and I offered suggestions at the end of each chapter. I now end by once again emphasizing its power.

There are endless more ways to be mindful. Throughout each day, we experience many spectacular visual moments. However, we rarely allow them to resonate. If we allow ourselves to be more aware, we can so easily turn them into Mindful Moments. I discussed the flower at the beginning of this book. I know how incredibly trite it sounds to say, "Stop and smell the roses," but this experience is more powerful than simply smelling a rose. This moment is timeless and can be awe inspiring. Take a moment and contemplate how many times in history a human has smelled a rose. Or pause and think about the complexity of that rose. How does it grow? How does it develop a smell? How does it become that color? Any of those questions allow a short pause for mindfulness.

When was the last time you fully appreciated a gorgeous sunset? A hummingbird? Did you allow yourself to leave your state of mind and fully appreciate the beauty? Try it. Allow a Mindful Moment, and see how it changes your entire mood. In order for it to be fully effective, be in the moment for at least ten seconds.

You can also consciously seek out those moments anytime you are feeling stressed. Nature is always around you. These moments can be found in the sky, in animals, birds, music, the taste of food, or even just an unusual texture. Mindfulness heightens all of our senses. Focus can occur through feeling something, seeing it, smelling it, or tasting it.

Ram Dass suggests "sky-gazing." Lie down on your back, look up at the sky, and watch the clouds pass over. He predicts that after a while, you will begin to experience the sky as a symbol of your awareness.[59] Feel yourself become a part of the clouds, floating with them. Feel them. Smell them. Listen to them. Once you train yourself to become calmed by the sky, you can simply look up to it when you need to lower stress. It will become an automatic response. The best part? The sky is always there, and at no cost.

Interestingly, walking can also be a form of mindfulness. Taking a short walk (or a long one) can change your entire perspective. Instead of walking to "get somewhere" or even to exercise, try walking for meditation. With each step, take in as much of your surroundings as

---

59 Ram Dass, *Still Here: Embracing Aging, Changing, and Dying* (New York, NY: Riverhead Books, 2000).

you can. Feel the world. The entire world. The universe. All in a breath. As I have mentioned before, everything you desire is no further than your breath.

These are a few other methods for mindfulness:

- Driving your car can be the most stressful of all daily activities. Become aware of your physical tensions. Where are your knees? Your hands? Your elbows? Where do you feel tension? Pay attention to your breathing.

- When you arrive to work, or home, or to the store, walk from your car with a new consciousness. You decide what that means for you.

- Begin a new ritual when you arrive home. Be aware of your surroundings and the people who may be there. Sit in peace for a few minutes. If you live alone, cherish that quiet new environment. What do you hear in the silence?

- It goes without saying that if you have a pet, all you have to do is absorb the love they present every time you arrive home. Feel it. Feel that love.

Prayer is probably the most popular form of mindfulness, practiced by millions of people around the world. My father certainly didn't believe in the "hocus pocus" of meditation, but on any given day, he might say, "C'mon, kids. Let's say the rosary." What could be more meditative or mindful than repeating a single prayer fifty times? That is the exact basis of meditation. The only thing missing is the breath, but that would often come when one of us kids gasped at the idea of the rosary.

Prayer is a beautiful way of expelling energy into the world; ask for good thoughts to bless yourself or others. Prayer is usually sincere and filled with hope. Energy. Beauty. Hope. Prayer.

We basically have a computer running full speed in our heads at every waking moment (and almost as often while sleeping). Finding peace is the goal. Once we are blessed to find that peace, we can allow the beautiful results of clarity, positive energy, compassion, and courage.

None of this is new information. We have always been told that if we believe, we will be successful. We will act with confidence and exude success. It only makes sense. We can write journals of hope, make small notes to ourselves to tell us we are good (and darn it, people like us), recite short daily affirmations, and many other ways of repeating patterns to our brain . . . all of which are being mindful. Consciously and unconsciously, we can unlock the mysteries of our mind simply by focusing.

There is a beautiful parable of a Chinese farmer:

Once upon a time there was a Chinese farmer whose horse ran away. That evening, all of his neighbors came around to commiserate. They said, "We are so sorry to hear your horse has run away. This is most unfortunate." The farmer said, "Maybe." The next day, the horse came back, bringing seven wild horses with it, and in the evening everybody came back and said, "Oh, isn't that lucky. What a great turn of events. You now have eight horses!" The farmer again said, "Maybe."

The following day, his son tried to break one of the horses, and while riding it, he was thrown and broke his leg. The neighbors then said, "Oh dear, that's too bad," and the farmer responded, "Maybe." The next day, the conscription officers came around to conscript people into the army, and they rejected his son because he had a broken leg. Again all the neighbors came around and said, "Isn't that great!" Again, he said, "Maybe."

The whole process of nature is an integrated process of immense complexity, and it's really impossible to tell whether anything that happens in it is good or bad—because you never know what will be the consequence of the misfortune; or, you never know what will be the consequences of good fortune.[60]

This parable is a great reflection of the first exercise in this book, creating your auto-graph. We have ups and downs in our lives, and when we map it onto a chart, we see that each one led us to the next one. We go way down and cannot find hope, and then something comes from those lows that brings a new life. As the parable says, you never know the consequences of good or bad.

We are most comfortable when we live in the mystery of what life will hand us. We don't judge the bad or obsess on the good; we walk in the balance.

---

60 Alan Watts, *The Way of Zen* (New York, NY: Pantheon Books, 1957).

REFERENCES

Alcoholics Anonymous Big Book. New York, NY: AA World Services, 1939.

American Journal of Preventive Medicine, *Social Media Use and Perceived Social Isolation Among Young Adults in the US*, July 1, 2018, https://www.ncbi.nlm.nih.gov/pmc/articles/PMC5722463/

Amin, Amid, "The 31 Benefits of Gratitude You Didn't Know About: How Gratitude Can Change Your Life," HappierHuman.com. August 1, 2020. https://www.happierhuman.com/benefits-of-gratitude/.

Archer-Smith, Eva, www.evaarcchersmith.com.

Aymee, Coget, PhD, *Happiness for Humankind Playbook*. San Francisco, CA, 2020.

B., Reggie, "How to Open Yourself to Your Life's Purpose," Oprah.com.

Bareham, Rev. Olivia Rosemarie, *Sacred Crossings*. Los Angeles, CA. www.sacredcrossings.com.

Bloom, Amy, "What If You're Afraid of Change," Oprah.com, November 2009, https://www.oprah.com/spirit/what-to-do-if-youre-scared-of-change.

Breuing, Loretta Graziano, PhD, *Habits of a Happy Brain*. Avon, MA: Adams Media, 2016.

Brown, Brené, PhD, LMSW, *Men, Women & Worthiness*, Boulder, CO: Audio CD, Sounds True (2012).

Brown, Brené, PhD, LMSW. *Daring Greatly*. New York, NY: Penguin Random House, 2012.

Brown, Brené, PhD, LMSW, *Gifts of Imperfection; Let Go of Who You Think You're Supposed to Be and Embrace Who You Are*. Center City, MN, Hazelden Publishing, 2020.

Bry, Barbara and Neil Sentura, "Investing in Happiness A Profitable Pursuit." *San Diego Union-Tribune* (San Diego, CA), January 5, 2015.

Canisius College, "Laughter is the Best Medicine," *Science Daily*, www.sciencedaily.com, January 26, 2008.

Carstensen, Laura, psychologist, director of Stanford Center of Longevity, *What Makes Older People Happier?*, TEDxWomen, 2011.

Centers for Disease Control and Prevention, *Well-Being Concepts*, https://www.cdc.gov/hrqol/wellbeing.html.

Cheu, Richard, *Living Well with Chronic Illness, A Practical and Spiritual Guide*, Indianapolis, IN: Dog Ear Publishing, 2013.

Chihuly, Dale, www.Chihuly.com, www.chihulygardenandglass.com.

Chirban, John T., PhD, "Seven Qualities of True Self: The Essence of Human Being," *Psychology Today*, August 14, 2013.

Clifford, Christine, *Not Now, I'm Having A No Hair Day*, Minneapolis, MN: University of Minnesota Press, www.CancerClub.com, 1996.

Close, Glenn, www.moviequotes.com, March 9, 2014.

Coget, Aymee, PhD, *Happiness for Humankind Playbook; Sustainable Happiness in 5 Steps*, Happiness for Humankind Publishing, 2020.

Corsini, R. J., and D. Wedding, *Current Psychotherapies*, Belmont, CA: Brooks/Cole, 2008.

Dalai Lama, and Howard C. Cutler, MD, *The Art of Happiness*, New York, NY: Riverhead Books, London, Penguin Books Ltd, 1998.

Dass, Ram, *Still Here: Embracing Aging, Changing, and Dying*, New York, NY: Riverhead Books, 2000.

Davidson, Sara, *LEAP, What Will We Do with the Rest of Our Lives?*, New York, NY: Ballantine Books, Random House Publishing Group, 2008.

DeBrule, Althea, "How to Find Your Calling in Life," Demand Media, Inc., www.eHow.com, 2010.

Ensler, Eve, *The Vagina Monologues*, New York, NY: Dramatists Play Service, Inc., 2000.

Fazang (Fa-tsang), A leading figure of medieval Chinese Buddhism, 643–712 CE.

Felleman, Ben, PhD, Behavioral Medicine Services of San Diego, www.bmedsandiego. com

Finch, Cindy, *A Problem with How We Treat Cancer–And How to Fix It*, Los Angeles, CA: LA Times, Opinion L.A., January 30, 2015.

Foley, Lyn, *Go Anyway; Sailing Around the World with Parkinson's*, Round Top, TX: Round Top Books, 2012, www.LynFoley.com.

Fortang, Laura Berman, *Now What? 90 Days to a New Life Direction*, London WC2R ORL: Penguin Books, Ltd, England, 2005.

Frankl, Viktor E., *Man's Search For Meaning*, Boston, MA: Beacon Press, 1959.

Freedman, Marc, *ENCORE: Finding Work that Matters in the Second Half of Life*, New York, NY: Public Affairs, 2007.

Gallup World Poll, Global Happiness Center, *World Happiness Report*, 2022.

Geoffreys, Clayton, *Kevin Love: The Inspiring Story of One of Basketball's Dominant Power Forwards*, Winter Park FL: Calvintir Books, LLC, 2016.

Gruver, Kathy, PhD, LMT, RM, *Conquer Your Stress with Mind/Body Techniques*, West Conshohocken, PA: Infinity Publishing, 2013.

Hall, Stephen, "The Cancer Lottery," *MIT Technology Review*, December 12, 2016, https://www.technologyreview.com/2016/12/12/69360/the-cancer-lottery/.

Hamilton, Scott, and Ken Baker, *How to be Happy (Even when you have every reason to be miserable)*, Nashville, TN: Thomas Nelson, 2008.

Hanson, Rick, PhD, *Hardwiring Happiness; The New Brain Science of Contentment, Calm, and Confidence*, New York, NY: Harmony Books, 2013.

Harper Neeld, Elizabeth, PhD, *Tough Transitions, Navigating Your Way Through Difficult Times*, New York NY: The Abbey of Gethsemani, New Directions Publishing Corp, Time Warner Book Group, 2005.

Harvard T. H. Chan School of Public Health, "Optimism Lengthens Life," *The Harvard Gazette*, June 8, 2022.

Hawter, Pende, Buddhist monk, founder of Karuna *Healing: A Tibetan Buddhist Perspective*, www.buddhanet.net/tib_heal.htm, 1995.

Hay, Louise, and David Kessler, *You Can Heal Your Heart; Finding Peace After a Breakup, Divorce, or Death,* Carlsbad, CA: Hay House, Inc., 2014.

Hoffman, Alice, *Survival Lessons*, New York, NY: Algonquin Books of Chapel Hill, Chapel Hill, NC, Workman Publishing, 2013.

Hollis, James, PhD, *Finding Meaning in the Second Half of Life*, New York NY: Gotham Books, 2005.

Institute for Brain Potential, Brian E. King, PhD, *The Habits of Happy People*, Los Banos, CA, 2014.

Isaacson, Walter, "Walker Percy's Theory of Hurricanes," *The New York Times Sunday Book Review*, August 4, 2015.

Johnson, Spencer, MD, *Who Moved My Cheese?*, New York, NY: G.P. Putnam's Sons, 1998.

Kingma, Daphne Rose, *The Ten Things to Do When Your Life Falls Apart, An Emotional and Spiritual Handbook*, Novato, CA: New World Library, 2010.

Kooden, Harold, PhD, *Golden Men: The Power of Gay Midlife*, New York, NY: Avon Books, 2000.

Kubler-Ross, Elisabeth, *On Death and Dying*, New York, NY: Scribner, 1969.

Lamott, Anne, "Becoming the Person You Were Meant to Be: Where to Start," Oprah.com, November 2009, https://www.oprah.com/spirit/how-to-find-out-who-you-really-are-by-anne-lamott/.

Leider, Richard, *Discovering What Matters, Workbook*, New York: MetLife Mature Market Institute, Metropolitan Life Insurance Company, 2009.

LeShan, Lawrence, PhD, *Cancer as a Turning Point: A Handbook for People with Cancer, Their Families, and Health Professionals*, Harmondsworth, England: Plume, 1990.

Lets Kick Ass, AIDS Survivor Syndrome, www.letskickass.org.

Lyubomirsky, Sonja, *The How of Happiness; A New Approach to Getting the Life You Want*, New York, NY: The Penguin Press, 2008.

Markova, Dawna, *I Will Not Die An Unlived Life*, York Beach, ME: Red Wheel/Weiser, LLC, 2000.

Marrs, Donald, *Executive in Passage, Career in Crisis: The Door to Uncommon Fulfillment*, Los Angeles, CA: Barrington Sky Publishing, 1990.

Martin, Demetri, *This Is a Book*, New York, NY: Hachette Book Group, 2011

Maurer, Robert, PhD, *One Small Step Can Change Your Life: The Kaizen Way*, New York, NY: Workman Publishing Co., 2004.

Metro-Golden-Mayer, *The Wizard of Oz*, Screenplay by Noel Langley, Florence Ryerson, and Edgar Allan Woolf, 1939.

Mitchell, Stephen, *The Enlightened Mind*, New York, NY: HarperPerennial, a division of Harper Collins Publishers, 1991.

National Institute of Mental Health, "Anxiety Disorders," https://www.nimh.nih.gov/health/statistics/any-anxiety-disorder

Neff, Kristin, PhD, *Self-Compassion: Stop Beating Yourself Up and Leave Insecurity Behind*, New York, NY: William Morrow, 2011.

Progoff, Ira, *Jung, Synchronicity, And Human Destiny*, New York, NY: Dell Publishing Company, 1978.

Queen Latifa, Produced by Lucian Piane and Marc Shaiman, Lyrics by Jason Lynn and Paul Broucek, "I Know Where I've Been," *Hairspray, The Musical*, 2002.

Riggenbach, Jeff, PhD, LPC, *The CBT Toolbox: A Workbook for Clients and Clinicians*, Eau Claire, WI: PESI Publishing and Media, 2013.

Rihanna, Album *Talk That Talk*, New York, NY: Def Jam Recordings, 2011.

Shipp, Josh, *Jump Ship: Ditch Your Dead-End Job and Turn Your Passion into a Profession*, New York, NY: St. Martin's Press, 2013.

Sokol, Jacob, life and leadership coach, founder of Sensophy Life Coaching, Brooklyn, New York, https://www.sensophy.com.

Sophocles (497/6-406/5 BC) Ancient Greek tragedian playwright.

St. Maarten, Anthon, *The Sensible Psychic*, Indigo House, 2002.

Star, Tamara, "7 Habits of Chronically Unhappy People," *HUFF POST Women, The Blog*, November 18, 2014.

Susskind, Andrew, MSW, SEP, CGP, *From Now On*, Los Angeles, CA: www.andrewsusskind.com, 2014.

Suttie, Jill, PhD, "Four Keys to Well-Being That May Help You Live Longer," *Greater Good Magazine*, April 13, 2022.

Taylor, Madisyn, *Unmedicated: The Four Pillars of Natural Awareness*, New York, NY: Atria Books, 2018; "Being Truly Thankful," "Beyond Counting Blessings," DailyOM. com; https://www.madisyntaylor.com/wp/.

Tolle, Eckhart, *The Power of NOW: A Guide to Spiritual Enlightenment*, Novato, California: Namaste Publishing and New World Library, 1999.

(The) Walt Disney Company, "The Bare Necessities," *The Jungle Book* movie. Lyrics by Terry Gilkyson, sung by Phil Harris, all rights reserved, 1967.

Watts, Alan, *The Way of Zen*, New York, NY: Pantheon Books, 1957.

Winfrey, Oprah, www.Oprah.com

Wolters, Lynda, *Voices of Cancer*, Herndon, VA: Mascot Books, 2019.

Wood, Alex M., et al., "The Role of Gratitude in the Development of Social Support, Stress, and Depression," *Journal of Research in Personality*, Science Direct, 2021.

Yalom, Irvin D., *Love's Executioner,* New York, NY: HarperCollins, HarperPerennial, 1990.

INDEX